HEALING ENERGY: WHOSE ENERGY IS IT?

RANDY CLARK
AND
SUSAN THOMPSON

Endorsements

The problem of true and false "miraculous" healings plagued the church even during the ministries of Jesus and the apostles Peter and Paul. Typically, the traditional church's reaction to this conflict is to take the bait of Satan and reject all supernatural manifestations - both false and true. Randy Clark's Healing Energy: Whose Energy Is It? takes the biblical response: it exposes the works of Reiki and other forms of New Age counterfeit claims to God's power, while affirming genuine works of the Spirit of Christ Jesus around the world today. Clark effectively demonstrates the historical, theological and practical differences between the trendy New Age "healing energies" versus the demonstrably true expression of the Gospel of our Lord Jesus Christ, delivered ever since: "by word and deed, by the power of signs and wonders, by the power of the Spirit of God" (Romans 15:18-19 ESV).

Jon Ruthven, Ph.D.
Professor Emeritus, Theology, Regent University
Doctor of Ministry Mentor, United Theological Seminary
Author: *On the Cessation of the Charismata* (2011) and *What's Wrong with Protestant Theology: Traditions vs. Biblical Emphasis* (2013)

Randy Clark is right; the modern popular brands of healing in the West become possible through the secularization of nature that occurs in late Scholasticism. When nature is credited with autonomy the results are philosophical nihilism or pantheism, a divinized nature. Clark expounds on the latter and its many incarnations, such as Esotericism, Theosophy, New Thought, New Paganism, New Age, Reiki and Therapeutic Touch, among others.

Clark counters what he estimates as aberrant forms of healing by recovering the Christian doctrine of Divine Healing as part of a comprehensive theology of salvation and as a manifestation of the Kingdom of God, both as reality and sign. Locating the problem in worldview,

Endorsements

Clark's corrective seeks to recover the Christian doctrine of Divine Healing by reconstructing a scripturally sound worldview that identifies a sovereign creator God over a limited, dependent creation that is both visible and invisible. A scriptural worldview not only accounts for realities visible and invisible but also demonstrates the joint interaction between the two, eliminating a closed-system of nature and a post-apostolic cessation of charismata.

At the heart of such a worldview is the Son of God, who mediates Heaven on earth and releases the fullness of the Kingdom of God in the hearts of people through the baptism of the Holy Spirit. The result is Divine Healing in all aspects extending from the spirit to the body.

Randy writes as a revivalist and practitioner who not only believes the doctrine of historic Christian doctrine of Divine Healing but also prays for it, expects it and sees it manifest in the church and in the mission field around the world.

Peter Bellini, Ph.D.
Assistant Professor in the Practice of Missiology
in the Vera Blinn Chair
Director of Non-Degree Programs, United Theological Seminary
Ordained Elder in the West Ohio Conference of
the United Methodist Church
Author: *Truth Therapy and Participation: Epistemology and Mission Theology*

Many Christians have been unwittingly duped by non-Christian healing methodologies and philosophies in pseudo-Christian dress. Healing Energy: Whose Energy Is It? is a vital expose of the dangerous New Age roots of alternative healing techniques. Randy Clark demonstrates how inadequate Christian views of healing have caused people to seek healing outside of biblical means. He has shown keen discernment in

Endorsements

clearly distinguishing biblical Christian healing from subtle counterfeits that often use Christian language. I highly recommend this book for its clarity of discernment, backed up by Scripture, sound doctrine, and Randy's first-hand experiences with genuine biblical healing.

Paul L. King, D.Min., D.Th.
2006 Scholar of the Year, Oral Roberts University
Doctor of Ministry Mentor, United Theological Seminary
Author: *Only Believe* and *God's Healing Arsenal*

The Book of Revelation shows that in the End Times occult activities would be widespread throughout the world, as we see today (Revelation 9:21; 21:8; 22:15). Randy Clark's book, Healing Energy: Whose Energy Is It? is an excellent, simple overview of how Christian healing differs from New Age Healing practices, which even many deceived Christians are practicing today, thinking that Christ's power is released through deceptively veiled pagan practices. This book takes a large amount of complicated information about New Age Healing versus Christian healing and theology and simplifies it for the average believer. In the face of New Age healing claims, the healing testimonies at the end of the book are a witness of the superior power of Jesus to forgive sin, heal the sick, and raise the dead today.

Gary S. Greig, Ph.D.
Adjunct Professor, United Theological Seminary
Author: *The Kingdom and the Power*

With an ever increasing hunger for the supernatural and manifest power, it is easy for the world, even the church, to be led astray in that which is masked with what would appear to be Christianity. Randy

Endorsements

Clark's newest book Healing Energy: Whose Energy Is It is a needed tool to educate and arm the church with knowledge of the various healing modalities and their origins that are in practice every day, even in what is becoming so popular as alternative medicine. There is only one true Healer and His name is Jesus Christ. This book is a must read for everyone!

Che' Ahn, D.Min.
Senior Pastor, HRock Church, Pasadena, CA
President, Harvest International Ministry
International Chancellor, Wagner Leadership Institute

Randy has seen and experienced God's healing in incredible ways. In Healing Energy: Whose Energy Is It?, he helps us to understand the difference between Christian healing and the practice found in New Age, Reiki, and other present day models. He cuts to the core to reveal the truth about healing and it's Source. It is time for the Church to step into its destiny and to release the healing power available in Jesus. Today is the day for blind eyes to see, deaf ears to open, and the lame to spring forth in dance. As you tap into the true Source of healing found in Jesus, may healing be released in even greater measures wherever you go.

Heidi Baker, Ph.D.
Founding Director of Iris Global
Author: *There is Always Enough*

In Healing Energy: Whose Energy Is It? Randy Clark effectively explains how Reiki therapy and Therapeutic Touch originally emerged from occult roots, but later gained considerable popularity in Western culture thinly disguised as "Christian" healing practices. He argues quite cogently that these two New Age healing modalities have little

Endorsements

support in the findings of natural science, have no basis of support in Christian belief, are for the most part ineffective, and encompass a world view which is totally at odds with Christianity. In contrast, the author provides many convincing examples of how he has personally witnessed blind eyes opening, deaf ears hearing, the lame walking and the dead being raised through the healing power of Jesus Christ. I heartily recommend this book to anyone interested in supernatural healing and its true origins.

Richard M. Riss, Ph.D.
Professor of History and Director of Academic Assessment
Somerset Christian College, Newark, NJ

As one of the few voices connecting and embracing both the healing movement and the academy, Randy Clark has an important message that draws on the strengths of both. In Healing Energy: Whose Energy Is It? Randy works to distinguish the theology behind Christian healing from the ideas behind other forms of spiritual healing. A natural implication of his presentation is that a culture that welcomes various other forms of spiritual healing should certainly welcome Christian healing no less.

Craig Keener, Ph.D.
Author: *Miracles: The Credibility of the New Testament Accounts*

HEALING ENERGY:
WHOSE ENERGY IS IT?

RANDY CLARK AND SUSAN THOMPSON

GLOBAL AWAKENING 1451 CLARK STREET MECHANICSBURG PA 17055

Healing Energy: Whose Energy Is It? by Randy Clark and Susan Thompson
© Copyright 2013 Randy Clark 1st Edition, June 2013. All rights reserved.

Edited by: Susan Thompson, Vicki West, and Bob Baynard

No part of this book may be reproduced, stored or transmitted in any form or by any means, electronic or mechanical, including photocopying and recording, or by any information storage or retrieval system, except as may be expressly permitted in writing by the publisher. Requests for permission should be addressed in writing to:

globalawakening

Apostolic Network of Global Awakening
1451 Clark Street
Mechanicsburg, PA 17055

For more information on how to order this book or any of the other materials that Global Awakening offers, please contact the Global Awakening Bookstore.

All scripture quotations, unless otherwise indicated, are taken from the Holy Bible, New International Version®, NIV®. Copyright ©1973, 1978, 1984, 2011 by Biblica, Inc.™ Used by permission. New International Version and NIV are trademarks registered in the United States Patent and Trademark Office by Biblica, Inc.™

Scripture quotations marked NASB are taken from the NEW AMERICAN STANDARD BIBLE®, Copyright © 1960,1962,1963,1968,1971,1972,1973,1975,1977,1995 by The Lockman Foundation. Used by permission.

Scripture quotations marked HCSB are taken from the Holman Christian Standard Bible®, Copyright © 1999, 2000, 2002, 2003, 2009 by Holman Bible Publishers. Used by permission. Holman Christian Standard Bible®, Holman CSB®, and HCSB® are federally registered trademarks of Holman Bible Publishers.

Scripture quotations marked (NLT) are taken from the Holy Bible, New Living Translation, copyright © 1996, 2004, 2007 by Tyndale House Foundation. Used by permission of Tyndale House Publishers, Inc., Carol Stream, Illinois 60188. All rights reserved.

Scripture quotations marked RSV/NRSV are from New Revised Standard Version Bible, copyright © 1989 National Council of the Churches of Christ in the United States of America. Used by permission. All rights reserved.

ISBN: 978-1-937467-56-2

This book is dedicated to the "one I love,"
DeAnne, my wife and best friend.

TABLE OF CONTENTS

ACKNOWLEDGEMENTS		15
FOREWORD		17
INTRODUCTION		23
CHAPTER 1	HOW THE CHURCH LOST THE POWER TO HEAL	29
CHAPTER 2	SEEDS PLANTED	37
CHAPTER 3	NEW AGE OR COSMIC HUMANISM: ITS ORIGINS AND WORLDVIEW	43
	Theosophy	44
	New Thought	47
	American Transcendentalism	50
	Neopaganism	51
CHAPTER 4	ENERGY HEALING MODALITIES: REIKI AND THERAPEUTIC TOUCH	59
	Reiki	61
	Therapeutic Touch	65
CHAPTER 5	CHRISTIAN HEALING	73
	The New Covenant	76
	The Atonement	78
	The Message of the Kingdom of God	79
CHAPTER 6	WHO'S ENERGY IS IT	83
	Reiki Energy	85
	Therapeutic Touch Energy	85
	Theistic or Pantheistic Energy	86
CHAPTER 7	EXAMINING THE EVIDENCE	95

The Doctrine of Creation versus Eternal Matter/Pantheism and the Doctrine of God's Nature (personal) versus Non-personal	96
The Doctrine of the Human Being (Personhood) versus 'Same' as God	97
The Doctrine of Time (linear) versus Circular (reincarnation)	98
The Doctrine of the Resurrection versus Reincarnation	100
The Doctrine of Sin versus Sin and Evil Are Only Illusions	100
The Doctrine of Salvation versus Unity with the 'One'	101
The Doctrine of Jesus' Incarnation as Historical versus Non-historical; Separate the Man Jesus from the Christ Spirit; Jesus' Lordship as the Way versus the 'Way Shower'	102
The Doctrine of the Second Coming as Reality versus Not a Reality	103
The Doctrine of Justice (Grace) versus Karma	104
The Doctrine of Impartation 'Comes to Us' versus 'Is Within Us'	105
CHAPTER 8 GOD HEALS TODAY	109
CONCLUSION	117
BIBLIOGRAPHY	127

Acknowledgement

I want to thank Susan Thompson for her work in helping me write this book. She took hundreds of pages of notes on various related subjects on New Age and Christian healing, as well as PowerPoints and DVDs of my teachings, and edited them into the final project. This book would not exist without her making sense out of my many writings on various subjects pertaining to New Age and Christian healing. I would not have had the time to write this book without her assistance due to the demanding speaking schedule I face.

I also want to thank Vicki West, one of my personal assistants, for her eye for detail and her help editing this book. Having a fresh set of eyes is always important.

I appreciated the valuable recommendations from Dr. Gary Greig near the end of the writing process, and for allowing me to quote from our personal emails on the subject of the New Age. Thank you, Gary, for being an encourager to me in ministry and writing.

I thank Bob Baynard, director of our bookstore and new product development for helping get this book through the publishing process.

Randy Clark

FOREWORD

It is my great honor and delight to write the "Foreword" for Randy Clark's new book *Healing Energy: Whose Energy Is It?* I am an academic theologian and met Randy Clark in 2010 at his School of Healing and Impartation in Michigan. While visiting my son, who did his graduate work in the area, my spouse Jane suggested I attend Randy's conference. It was a divine appointment. The Holy Spirit immediately connected us and we have since developed a blessed friendship. Having taught in mainline seminaries since 1987, I had not heard of Randy prior to 2010.

God has placed in Randy a heart for transforming theological education and as a result Randy prays for opportunities to impact seminary education. Together Randy and I are able to cooperate for the future of God's work. Meeting and working with Randy has transformed my seminary instruction. Before meeting Randy, I taught inner healing of the wounded only, overlooking physical and spiritual healing. Now I teach holistic healing, including physical healing, in my classrooms. Randy's books are part of my curriculum and my students love them. I see this book as an informative and useful resource for my students, who desire to know the difference between Christian healing and the healing that is promoted by non-Christian groups.

I am sincerely grateful to Randy for publishing such a significant and practical theological book. I have found Randy a genuinely compassionate, considerate, and non-judgmental human being, but one not afraid to sharply and passionately explicate the fundamental differences between Christian healing and New Age energy healing practices. He has written a rare and unique book that illuminates a challenging subject with spiritual discernment.

It is obvious and wonderful that God has called and used Randy to impart the anointing of the Holy Spirit to His Church for her renewal for our generation. God has supernaturally healed Randy several times and uses him as a humble and potent wounded healer. The Holy Spirit bestowed upon him three intense impartations; the first one so vigorous that all of his joints ached after the power of the Holy Spirit ran through his body all night and the next day. The second impartation was so strong and painful that he feared his own death. It was comparable to the experience of the "dark night of the soul" for mystic St. John of the Cross (1542-1591). After the third impartation, major outpourings of the Holy Spirit occurred in the Vineyard and other churches.

In 1994, John Arnott of the Airport Vineyard Christian Fellowship in Toronto, Canada invited Randy for four nights of meetings starting on January 20th. Those four nights were extended to 12.5 years by the extravagantly unprecedented outpouring of the Holy Spirit. This event became known as the Toronto Blessing, through which God has touched an estimated 1.8 million pastors, leaders, and individuals from approximately two hundred countries. The Toronto Blessing marked a turning point in the history of the Church and was one of the largest and longest outpourings of the Holy Spirit in history. The sovereign visitation of the Holy Spirit fell with particular strength on Randy and others who have since become leaders in the mighty worldwide move of the Holy Spirit that continues today (*Lighting Fires*, xvii).

Randy is an extraordinary and charismatic healer who has literally reshaped the map of world religion by expanding the population of Christians around the globe under the sovereign guidance of the Holy Spirit. Travelling tirelessly all over the world Randy has imparted this mighty outpouring of the Holy Spirit to others such as Rolland and Heidi Baker, Bill Johnson, Ché Ahn, Leif Hetland and Georgian and Winnie Banov, all of whom have become leaders in their own right, spreading the gospel with miracles, signs and wonders to almost every continent.

Based on biblical and historical foundations, Randy's theology is authentically wholesome, aligning his heart with God's heart as he seeks God's will first in his ministry. Randy is an able and competent theologian in his own right and this book is the good evidence of his sound theological scholarship. He beautifully highlights the purpose of Christian healing, which is to seek to proclaim God's reign on the earth by restoring His New Covenant through healing as it is found in the atonement of Jesus Christ, while reminding us that healing itself is not the ultimate purpose of the mission of the Church, but a sign that points beyond itself, showing the arrival of God's reign on the earth.

The theological contrasts between Christianity and New Age energy healing modalities that Randy has highlighted bear tremendous value for Christians and non-Christians alike who desire to understand these differences. While some New Age energy healing practices have been recognized by medical communities as legitimate healing agencies even to the point of being covered by medical insurance, their healing practices are rooted in spiritually abstruse resources. I believe the Holy Spirit stirred up Randy to write this book in order to reveal the realities of these cultic healing groups and warn the uninformed about their murky sides. Randy sounds the alarm to tolerant Christians who use these alternative healing methods without serious biblical reflection; however, he does not condemn them, but explores their identities as truthfully as possible. "Beloved, do not believe every spirit, but test the spirits to see whether they are from God" (1 John 4:1, NRS).

Randy succinctly contrasts the Christian worldview with the New Age worldview, walking the reader through the theistic doctrine of creation as distinguished from the pantheistic view of nature, examining resurrection versus reincarnation, and the issues of evil and sin as reality not illusion. While Christians seek salvation, those outside Christianity often pursue oneness with the universe as their ultimate salvation, with no appreciation of the grace of God beyond our own merits, holding instead to the principle of Karma, the law of cause and effect. Christians accept and confess Jesus as the Christ who is God while other healing groups regard Jesus as a christ, only one of many. Christians acknowledge God who is transcendent and immanent in us through impartation while New Age healing modalities only believe in the immanent divine within us.

Of great importance and central to this book is the discussion of the source of power as found in Christianity versus the power found in New Age energy healing practices. Christianity utterly relies on *the* personal God, whereas New Age healing modalities derive their healing power from impersonal cosmic energy. On the one hand, Randy emphasizes the personal relationship with God who heals us and restores God's own image in us and contrasts it with New Age healing practices that treat healing as the mere use of the impersonal energy of the cosmos.

Through this book Randy explains how important it is for the Church to restore her original power of healing. He cogently points out healing as an essential mission of Jesus and of His disciples. Randy himself is a meek and potent healer of God, but here his heart is filled with the passion of the Holy Spirit for the restoration of the original intention of Jesus' ministry of healing the sick and setting the captives free. He articulates how the Church has overlooked her mission of healing and how Christians and non-Christians, hungry for healing, have stretched their hands toward Reiki and Therapeutic Touch and other New Age healing practices. This book is a great contribution to the Church, explaining the worldviews of New Age healing practices in light of the theology of Christianity.

Randy is a wonderful human being, an authentic Christian, an astonishing Christian healer, a divinely appointed impartation leader, and a competent scholar in the field of healing. As a practitioner and scholar of Christian healing, Randy Clark is peerlessly qualified to write such a book as this. This book *Healing Energy: Whose Energy Is It?* has plainly demonstrated Randy's expertise in the area of New Age energy healing modalities while stating his own succinct theological positions. He has written more than a dozen books, and just as the apostle Paul led many to Christ, so Randy has also led countless many to Christ through his writings anointed by the power of the Holy Spirit. This seemingly thin book is a gift of the Holy Spirit that will guide many to the healing path of God's righteousness for the sake of Jesus' name while we make our way through the confusing valley of New Age energy healing practices.

Andrew S. Park, Ph.D.
Professor of Theology and Ethics
United Theological Seminary
Dayton, OH

INTRODUCTION

In 2007 I was invited to speak at a symposium that was sponsored by both the Medical School and the Divinity School of St. Louis University, which is a Catholic Dominican university. The title of the symposium was *Healing: Catholic, Protestant, and Medical Perspectives.* Over the course of the symposium I learned that there was a good deal of interest in the medical field regarding spiritual healing, especially Christian healing. To my surprise and dismay, a nearby Roman Catholic hospital, St. Anthony's, also had an interest in healing, especially non-Christian healing modalities similar to Reiki and Therapeutic Touch. Fast forward to 2013 and we see that the Catholic Church has taken a strong stand against non-Christian healing modalities like Reiki and Therapeutic Touch.

I came away from this symposium on healing eager to learn more about what the medical community was uncovering regarding the roots of sickness and the effects of faith upon disease. I was awakened by one of the lectures offered by a professor of psychiatry about the benefits of spirituality. I began to read whatever I could on this topic and by year's end I had read thousands of pages on the subject. The findings were exciting to me because they revealed a relationship between spirituality and health. What troubled me was the lack of discernment regarding the type of spirituality. Several authors stated that it didn't make any difference whether the spirituality was Hindu, Buddhist, Jewish, New Age, or Christian.

Armed with new information and more curious than ever, I began researching the differences between world religions and their spiritual and health-related benefits. I wanted to know if medical evidence exists that Christianity, with its rich history of healing, has more power to heal than the other world religions.

At one point in my research I discovered a 2005 Doctor of Ministry dissertation by Rhonda J. McClenton titled *Spirits of the Lesser Gods: A Critical Examination of Reiki and Christ-Centered Healing*.[1] Through her research, Dr. McClenton, a Christian, proved the ineffectiveness of Reiki as a healing therapy and highlighted its spiritual dangers. I was shocked at what Dr. McClenton's research had brought to light.

Then, in January of 2010, I came across another dissertation, this one on Reiki. It was submitted in 2009 as part of a Master of Arts degree program to the Faculty of the School of Theology of the University of the South in Sewanee, Tennessee. The author, Ruth Mayeux Allen, is a Reiki Master and the title of her dissertation is *Pneumatology: The Spirit of Reiki*.[2] As I read her dissertation it became obvious that its purpose was to become an apologetic for Reiki as a Christian practice. She had already introduced her training seminar on healing through Reiki in several Methodist and Episcopal churches in the United States. The dissertation contained quotes from many Christian theologians.

Concerned, I sent her quotes to a friend of mine, theologian Dr. Gary Greig. Dr. Greig's response was that Allen was quoting theologians and scriptures out of context and distorting their meaning in order to support her thesis that Reiki and Christian theology were compatible. Dr. Greig disagreed with Ruth Mayeux Allen's thesis and its conclusion.

The following year I became aware that in one of the states in the northeast, in order to become a licensed massage therapist or a chaplain, one must take a course on Reiki or Therapeutic Touch. I also became aware that many health insurance companies now cover the cost of treatment using energy healing therapies like Reiki and Therapeutic Touch.

Then, in 2011, while teaching on New Age and Christian healing modalities during one of my *Schools of Healing and Impartation*, I found myself bombarded with questions from people seeking clarity and discernment, and realized just how much interest and confusion exists on this topic. Many people asked if I had written a book on the subject, and it became increasingly clear that a book was needed.

While this is a book about religion, philosophy and theology, it is also an examination of the age-old battle between the Kingdom of God and the kingdom of this world from the perspective of healing. It is in the context of healing that New Age is attempting to win the allegiance of the hearts and minds of people, especially Christians, by presenting New Age energy healing therapies with a thin veneer of Christianity. As a result of this deception many people are engaging in New Age practices unaware of the spiritual dangers involved.

I encourage believers and non-believers alike to become educated about the energy healing modalities that are being offered today. In the following pages we will examine Reiki and Therapeutic Touch, two major New Age healing practices, and compare them to Christian models and practices of healing, with the goal of coming to a better understanding of the major worldviews and belief systems of the New Age Movement and Christianity. We will also examine the source and nature of energy as it is found in Christian healing and New Age healing modalities.

The purpose of this book is not to demonize those who have become involved in Reiki or Therapeutic Touch, but rather to clarify that the New Age worldview and its practices are inconsistent with the Christian worldview. Not everything offered to us is good, even if it masquerades as such. I believe that those who have become involved with New Age energy healing modalities have been deceived. They are good people, people who are aware of the spiritual side of life, people who are motivated by compassion to alleviate the suffering of others, and who do not believe in scientific reductionism that is void of the life of the spirit.

I believe that people become involved in these New Age practices because of noble and good motivations, and because many grew up in a form of Christianity that offered them no hope of seeing the power to heal through prayer ministry. The post-modern mind, with its hunger for transcendent spiritual experiences, has turned away from the Church that bears the name of Jesus Christ, the great physician, because the Church has so often offered no outlet for this hunger.

Endnotes

[1]Rhonda J. McClenton, *Spirits of the Lesser Gods*, 2007, Allen, *Pneumatology*, 2009.

[2]Ruth Mayeux Allen, *Pneumatology*, 2009.

CHAPTER ONE
HOW THE CHURCH LOST THE POWER TO HEAL

The early disciples of Jesus were for the most part a poorly educated group, lacking status in their society. Their religion was considered illegal. They had no money or facilities, none of the ingredients that we today would consider necessary to launch a world-changing movement, and yet in three hundred years they had Christianized the Roman Empire and established the Church. How did they do it? They did it through power – the power to cast out demons and heal the sick. They were not ashamed of the power of the good news they announced; the news that the power of another kingdom, the Kingdom of God, was now available to the followers of Jesus. It was this power that demonstrated the truth of the gospel and drew people to the Church. So just how did the powerful church of Jesus Christ lose its power?

The powerful Church of Jesus Christ lost its authority to serve in power, and its understanding of the gospel as the in-breaking of the Kingdom of God, through the gradual process of moving from theistic Christianity to deistic Christianity. As a result of this shift we abdicated the power to push back the dominion of the god of this world, the devil. The two most representative forms of the practical deistic version of Christianity are liberalism and cessationism. I am sure neither group would consider themselves as deists, but for practical purposes, their theology regarding the supernatural activity of God in the world through His gifts or energies ends up with a practical deistic outlook. Simply put, Deism is the worldview that God created the world like a clock, wound it up and now lets it run by itself without His interference. He remains beyond His creation. He does not break into it or break the perceived laws of nature, hence, no miracles.

Liberalism denies all miracles, believing they are not historical events, but myths and stories the Church created in order to present its faith. Liberal theology is based upon a scientific worldview of Newtonian physics in which the universe is a machine running on natural law; law which cannot and will not be broken by God. This rationalism came out of the Age of the Enlightenment. In recent times science has moved from Newtonian physics to quantum physics, and the world of matter and law has become the world of energy and mystery. The opposite theological pole from liberalism is fundamentalism, and almost all fundamentalists are cessationist.

Cessationism is the belief that all the healings and miracles in the Bible are historical. Cessationists believe that God did do miracles and perform healings through His Son and through the early disciples, but He did so in order to establish correct doctrine through the writings of the apostles, which eventually became the Bible. Once His correct doctrine was established, healings and miracles, tongues, and prophecies were no longer needed and so they ceased.

Furthermore, Cessationism says that if miracles and healings are still possible, then the canon of the Bible would not be closed - there could be more scriptures. But since the canon is closed, and miracles and healings were to authenticate the message and the messengers, then gifts of healing are no longer in existence. If this is true, then God rarely intervenes in response to intercessory prayer; interventions are not to be expected as normative but as rare exceptions to the norm. The mainline historical denominations have their roots in the Reformation, especially the Reformed (which is the theology of most Baptists), and Lutherans.

For the last five hundred years liberal and cessationist Protestant pastors have taught North American and European churches not to believe or expect the gifts of healing and working of miracles to exist in the Church. They have preached a powerless gospel.

The Roman Catholic Church never believed the gifts of healing and miracles had ended, but they developed a theology that took the ministry of healing out of the hands of the laity and put it exclusively in the hands of the clergy or the religious (monks and sisters) who were considered the only ones "holy" enough to minister healing. Furthermore, they put forth the doctrine of sickness as a means of sanctification; we have been told to "carry our cross" as Jesus did and in the process we will be sanctified.

Protestants, excluding Pentecostals and Charismatics, also believed sickness was for sanctification.[1] When you consider that seventy-five to eighty percent of Christians in Europe and North America were taught that the doctrine of healing has no true biblical support, is it any wonder that people have gone outside the Church to learn about healing? The Church is guilty of creating the spiritual context of impotency that has caused good people to become involved in alternative healing modalities such as Reiki and Therapeutic Touch.

On behalf of the Church, I ask you to forgive the Church and its leaders, myself included, for not providing the opportunity to learn about healing in your local church. We have so often failed to offer training in healing and the gifts of the Spirit, both in the local church and in our seminaries and Bible colleges. We have too often told you that the age of healing is over and that God does not heal anymore in response to prayer.

Many of us have taught that the gifts of healing no longer exist for the Church. And, if healing does occur, we have told you that it is not to be perceived as normative, but as a sovereign exception to the norm of living a life void of His power and intervention.

I want to say to all of you reading this book, "Please forgive us! We, the Church, are sorry for this deistic distortion of Christianity and the terrible impact it has had of inoculating many to the truth of the Gospel; a truth that doesn't consist of talk but in power; a truth that isn't based on human wisdom but on the power of God. We didn't know what we were doing and we are profoundly sorry."

As a representative of the Church, and of Christ, I want to ask you, the reader, to forgive the Church and her leadership for presenting and proclaiming a weak, neutered form of Christianity that does not look like the Christianity of the Bible. It is our fault so many have gone to New Age practices. We the Church have offered no outlet for the compassion and spiritual desire in people's hearts to experience the power of the spirit realm in order to bring relief to human suffering.

If we had been faithful to the Great Commission, and the commission of Jesus in the Bible, we would never have developed such a weak representation of Christianity. We would not have reduced the faith to doctrinal belief rather than an expectancy for God to move in power.

The Church has not been faithful to Jesus' Great Commission, especially the second half that says, "and teaching them to obey everything I have commanded you" (Matthew 28:20). At the top of the list of things the Church has failed at is the ministry of compassion expressed through healing the sick and liberating those who are demonized, while ministering to the poor and those that are broken-hearted. We have created a climate of spiritual impotency and as a result many have turned away from the Church to New Age practices and beliefs.

In addition to this climate of spiritual impotency, there is a realization of a growing dissatisfaction with modern allopathic medicine. This dissatisfaction is driving many to explore alternative medicine and practices. The National Center for Complementary and Alternative Medicine (NCCAM) says, "The 2007 National Health Interview Survey (NHIS), which included a comprehensive survey of CAM [complementary and alternative medicine] use by Americans, showed that approximately 38 percent of adults use CAM."[2]

"According to the 2007 National Health Interview Survey . . . more than 1.2 million adults - 0.5 percent of the U.S. general adult population - had used an energy healing therapy, such as Reiki, in the previous year."[3]

In an attempt to use science as the basis for all medical practice, allopathic medicine has reduced our humanity to tiny bits of chemicals and matter interacting with each other and in the process lost sight of the whole person. The picture of the interrelatedness of who we are as living souls, conjoined in body and spirit, has been lost. In essence, Western allopathic medicine seems to have lost its soul by negating the existence of our souls. We are now treated as a sickness or a disease rather than as a person. Surgery and pharmaceuticals have been promoted as the answer to all our ills.

This loss of self, experienced in the practice of modern medicine, doesn't resonate well within us, for each human being has an innate sense, given by our Creator God that we are more than mere accident, more than simply chemistry, more than mere flesh and bones. We are created in His image as integrated, whole persons. Swiss medical doctor Paul Tournier's book, *The Healing of Persons,* published in 1965, was a prophetic harbinger of the alienation patients were beginning to experience with doctors and care-givers.[4] Dr. Tournier was aware of the need to recognize our personhood in the process of healing our bodies.

With the dual failures of the Church and modern medicine to adequately address our spiritual and physical needs, conditions were ripe for the seeds of Western Esotericism, planted in the last quarter of the nineteenth century, to germinate. They found fertile ground in the counterculture of the 1960s and 1970s that rocked America.

Endnotes

[1](DeArteaga 1992) (Hyatt 1996) (Ruthven, *On the Cessation of the Charismata: The Protestant Polemic on Postbiblical Miracles*, 1993) (Ruthven, *What's Wrong With Protestant Theology?* 2013) (Clark, *School of Healing and Impartation: Deliverance, Disbelief, and Deception Workbook*, 2009; Workbook 2011)

[2]National Center for Complementary and Alternative Medicine Online, nccam.nih.gov "What is Complementary and Alternative Medicine," October 2008, Web, (accessed December 27, 2012).

[3]Ibid.

[4]Paul Tournier, *The Healing of Persons*, 1965.

CHAPTER TWO
SEEDS PLANTED

In the middle 1800s, a healing movement blossomed in America among Evangelical Protestant leaders. These were highly educated, well trained leaders of Baptist, Presbyterian, Dutch Reformed, and Congregationalist churches. Names like A.J. Gordon, A.B. Simpson, Andrew Murray, Charles Cullis and a host of others were championing the rediscovery of healing within Protestantism. The epicenter of all of this was in Boston, MA and it was connected to the rapid rise of the Holiness Movement.

The Holiness Movement broke away and came out of Methodism, primarily because many thought the Methodist Church was becoming too liberal, and was no longer true to her heritage and the emphasis on the experience of a second definite work of grace that followed justification, which came from Methodisim's founder John Wesley, and in America, Francis Asbury.

At the same time that this healing movement, known as the Faith Cure Movement, was blossoming, the seeds of what would later become the New Age Movement were emerging. The New Age Movement would also have an emphasis upon healing, and a Gnostic type theology that denied most of the important doctrines of Christianity. This New Age Movement was actually composed of two movements; Christian Science and Western Esotericism. Western Esotericism was made up of groups like Theosophy, New Thought, and Transcendentalism, all born in New England in the 19th century. The origins of Christian Science were later than the origins of the Protestant Faith Cure Movement.

The seeds that were planted through Western Esotericism began to bear fruit in the 1960s and 1970s with the rise of the hippie movement and its accompanying drug culture. Eastern religions began to flow into the hearts and minds of Westernized society through this drug culture. The musical *Hair* hit the top of the charts, and everyone was singing, "This is the dawning of the Age of Aquarius," even if they did not have a clue what the words meant. Actually a few did, but most did not. They just knew it was about change, and we, our generation, were going to be in the middle of it. We're still in the middle of that change. The professors that populate our universities today were the teens and twenty-somethings of the late 1960s and early 1970s.

Something else happened at this time, and that something was the Jesus Movement. Hundreds of thousands, if not millions of youth were experiencing the power of God, and many were called away from their planned vocations to enter the ministry. I was one of them. In 1970 I abandoned my desire to be a social studies teacher, which I had held on to since the 7th grade, and entered college to study for ministry. When I entered the Southern Baptist Theological Seminary in Louisville, Kentucky in September of 1974, it had the largest freshman class in its history.

All of this took place on the heels of the Charismatic Movement in America, which began on April 3, 1960, when Dennis Bennett, an Episcopal priest, reported "speaking in tongues" in his prestigious Episcopal Church in southern California. Suddenly, Christians in often stale, predictable, spiritually near-dead churches were experiencing the power of God. They were having visions and dreams, and speaking in tongues.

Within the Roman Catholic Church this new Pentecost began in 1967. But it did not break out among the poor or in tent meetings or store-front churches on the wrong side of the tracks as it had a little over a half century earlier, among Protestants in the Pentecostal Movement. No, for the Catholics, God chose to pour out His Spirit in their universities, among the highly educated.

With these three visitations of God, almost on top of each other, it seemed like the whole country was invaded by God. The real shocker for many in all of this was that God was revealing His grace, His mercy, His power, and His love, in great measure, to a bunch of drugged-out kids, the hippies. It seemed like the Haight-Ashbury section of San Francisco, which was the epicenter of the hippie movement, suddenly became the epicenter for a move of God that would eventually touch youth around the world. The "flower children" became His children. Even though they weren't crying out to Him, God himself heard their cry. They wanted peace, not war, and God gave them His Son, the Prince of Peace.

Soon, the hitchhiking hippies with their index and middle finger raised to give the peace sign were finding others who were hitchhiking, and they too had a sign, only it wasn't two fingers but one, the pointer finger pointing to what they believed was the "only" way to peace. They were pointing to Jesus.

Over time, hundreds of thousands of hippies would switch allegiance from drugs, sex, and rock and roll to Jesus. They would discover that instead of an altered state of consciousness brought on by drugs, they could receive a genuine and permanent altered state of consciousness from their heavenly Father. He made them new. He took a generation alienated from their parents at birth, when they were whisked from their mother's breasts to a bottle, a generation unbound to their parents and willing to receive the seeds of the enemy in their minds and bodies, and broke their rebellious hearts.

As these mighty moves of God collided with the New Age Movement, a philosophical and theological battle for the allegiance of the souls of hundreds of millions of people commenced, and it was not unlike the earlier battle waged for the minds and worship of Americans that occurred in the last quarter of the nineteenth century.

Both the New Age Movement and the Jesus Movement had a strong emphasis upon experience, especially the experience of spiritual realities, and both had a strong emphasis on healing. Both movements were primarily aimed at the youth of the nation - those in their late teens and early twenties. And both had been born out of a rejection of the staid, rules-driven, experience-barren form of Christianity that appealed to reason and to the brain, but left the heart mostly untouched.

Just as a century earlier, many of the key leaders of the movements that make up Western Esotericism had been raised in Christian homes. The same was true for the key leaders within the New Age Movement. They had been raised on a powerless faith. Victims of cessationism, they grew up within rationalistic liberal churches that didn't believe in miracles, or in historic reformation denominations that emphasized that miracles had once happened in the life of the Church but had ceased.

Whether raised in liberalism or cessationism, the fruit was the same; they had a form of godliness but were denying the power thereof. The New Age Movement had particular appeal to Evangelicals and Cessationists because of the pseudo-scientific way in which it presented its arguments.

CHAPTER THREE
NEW AGE OR COSMIC HUMANISM: ITS ORIGINS AND WORLDVIEW

The roots of the New Age Movement date back to the origins of Western Esotericism in the 14th century.[1] As the natural sciences emerged from the liberal arts, a secularization of nature emerged. Wouter Hanegraaff, a scholar of western esotericism and author of *New Age Religion and Western Culture* says that "a secularization of the cosmos at the expense of the sacred" occurred, making nature "an organic and lawful domain worthy of attention in its own right."[2]

This secularization of the cosmos,[3] this removing of the spiritual meaning from our existence, this stripping nature of its creator and reducing all things to accident and chance, and having no purpose, this quasi-deistic understanding, was replaced with a rationalistic scientism. This move opened the door for an examination, and eventual rejection by some, of the (liberal) Judeo-Christian worldview in favor of a reinterpretation that became the basis for Western esoteric thought. In essence, Esotericists believe that nature is a force in and of itself, to be interacted with through the practice of alchemy and other esoteric arts such as astrology and magic, in order to gain intimate knowledge that allows influence in the spiritual realms.[4]

43

There is no organized New Age religion, but rather a worldview that blends the occult with humanism and spirituality as found in Western Esotericism, and has a greater influence than that of Eastern religions. The Religious Movements Homepage Project website says this about the New Age Movement: "It has exercised a pervasive influence in Western society. Its occult and humanistic philosophy can be found in the entertainment media, global politics, environmental crusades, educational paradigms, alternative medical practices, and the world of business."[5]

The present-day New Age Movement is to a considerable extent based on the teachings of Helena Blavatsky, though some writers have described Alice Bailey as the founder of the "New Age Movement."[6] The term New Age was used prior to Bailey. A weekly journal of Christian liberalism and socialism called *The New Age* was published as early as 1894.[7] James R. Lewis and J. Gordon Melton, in *Perspectives on the New Age* have this to say: "The most important - though certainly not the only source of this transformative metaphor, as well as the term "New Age," was Theosophy, particularly as the Theosophical perspective was mediated to the movement by the works of Alice Bailey."[8] We will examine Theosophy in a moment.

The New Age Movement is vast and complex and this book is by no means an exhaustive study of it, but rather a brief overview of some aspects that will serve as a foundation for our examination of two energy healing therapies prominent in the New Age Movement. There are five groups that make up Western Esotericism: Theosophy, New Thought, American Transcendentalism, Neo-Paganism, and Occultism. Let's examine each one individually.

Theosophy

Theosophy originated in the 19th century and was deeply rooted in the spirit of anti-Christ, denying that Jesus was the Christ.[9] It is very anti-Christian, seeing Christianity as its enemy and the main belief system that stands against its [Theosophy's] replacement belief system. Theosophy aims to supplant Christianity.

Theosophy reinterprets most of the doctrines of Christianity in a heretical way, giving the same terms a very different unorthodox meaning. It has developed as an alternate spirituality/worldview to Christianity, emphasizing metaphysical beliefs of a heretical nature. Theosophy had much in common with Gnosticism, which was perhaps the first major heresy to threaten Christianity. Dr. R.T. Kendall states, "The New Age Movement is ancient Gnosticism in new dress."[10]

Theosophy in Greek means "divine wisdom" or "wisdom concerning God." Those who adhere to theosophic theology believe this divine wisdom is obtained "by the direct intuition of the Divine essence."[11] Theosophists consider themselves "to be in harmony with the central principle of the universe" and their "knowledge of the secret forces of nature of the true relation between the world and man frees them from the ordinary limitations of human life, and gives them a peculiar power over the hidden forces of the macrocosm."[12]

Theosophical theology forms part of the basis of New Age religion. It is a philosophy of life based on the tenants of reincarnation and the law of Karma, much like Hinduism. In theosophy there is no heaven or hell. Sin and the miseries of life are the product of our own ignorance, and they will gradually be redeemed through a series of reincarnations, until we are freed from earthly constrains and become "one" with the Absolute One. John Driscoll writing in the Catholic Encyclopedia, says this about Theosophy's theology: "As man advances in this process his spirit becomes stronger, and can develop latent powers, not shown in ordinary mortals."[13]

Modern theosophy finds its origins in the Theosophical Society which was established by Madame Blavatsky in New York City in 1875. Helena Petrovna Blavatsky was of Russian origin and spent much of her growing up years in the Ukraine in the home of her maternal grandmother. Here she had the opportunity to read through her grandmother's extensive library of books on medieval occultism, as is evidenced from her correspondence during that period.[14]

As a young woman from a family of financial means, she traveled extensively throughout Europe, the Middle East, and at one point Tibet and India, where she undertook an extended study of Tibetan Buddhism which is deeply occult. It was there that she claimed she received revelation from the Mahatmas for her writings, especially for her well-known book *The Secret Doctrine*, which details the tenants of Theosophy and its decidedly occult roots.[16] Blavatsky's detailed description of these revelations can be found in a number of her writings, many of which appeared in her monthly journal titled *Lucifer,* which she published in the late 1800s.[15]

During this same time period Blavatsky met Henry Olcott and together they founded the Theosophical Society in America, promoting Theosophy as *the* Occult Science, which they claimed has been preserved down through the ages by carefully selected and trained individuals who continue to practice these teachings.

Promoted as a "system of 'absolutist metaphysics'" Theosophy proposes a reconciliation of science, philosophy and religion "into a unified worldview," by attempting to blend concepts, vocabulary and theology from a variety of religious and philosophical traditions by amending "and explaining within an esoteric or occult framework" these various elements.[17] Wouter Hanegraaff clearly points out theosophy's syncretistic blend of eastern religions with occult practices that characterize Blavatsky's contributions to what is now loosely referred to as New Age religion.[18]

While factions of the New Age Movement promote their energy healing modalities as being like Christian healing, a close examination by scholars of Theosophy reveals little in the way of reconciliation and more in the way of annihilation when it comes to Christian theology. Theosophy is the root of Therapeutic Touch, one of the energy healing modalities that we will examine later in this book. Wouter Hanegraaff is quite specific in describing the New Age disposition towards Christianity when he says, "As a religious movement, spiritualism was characterized by a pronounced scientistic attitude combined with a vehement opposition to institutionalized Christianity."[19] In other words, some of this vehement opposition sprang from the argument by theosophists and spiritualists that Christianity was rife with sectarianism because of its distinction between those who believe in the tenants of the Christians faith and those who don't.[20] In their mind, in the absence of sin and evil, there is no need for the redemption offered through Jesus Christ as found in Christianity.

Author J. Gordon Melton, considered by some to be an apologist for the alternative religions and cults he writes about, characterizes the Theosophical Society as a "major force in the dissemination of occult literature in the West in the twentieth century."[21]

New Thought

The New Thought movement came out of the romanticism of the 19th century, combined with a quest for the metaphysical, and in reaction to religious liberalism, with the skepticism that pervaded the 18th century. Those who subscribe to New Thought theology believe that "the spirit is more real and more powerful than matter, and that the mind has the power to heal the body."[22] There are elements of Hinduism, Platonism, Swedenborgianism, and Hegelianism in New Thought, blended with an amended view of Christianity that veers significantly from the basic tenants of the Christian faith.[23]

New Thought promotes the divinity of all human beings in addition to the divinity of Jesus. It declares that we attain salvation in this life, and that heaven and hell are states of consciousness rather than actual places.[24] In New Thought theology, God is ubiquitous in a pantheistic sense. In other words, all of nature is divine (god).

The three major groups that make up the New Thought movement are the Unity Church, which was founded in 1891 by Charles and Myrtle Fillmore, the United Church of Religious Science founded by Ernest Holmes in 1927, and Divine Science, which was founded in the later part of the 19th century by Emma Hopkins, a student of Mary Baker Eddy, founder of Christian Science.[25]

Charles and Myrtle Fillmore, founders of the Unity Church, struggled throughout their marriage with Myrtle's illnesses, until she became well after praying. As a result of Myrtle's healing, Charles embarked on a quest to study religion and philosophy and the connection between science and religion. They began to write and publish their findings and eventually established the Unity Church.[26]

Ernest Holmes, founder of the United Church of Religious Science, did not have a personal experience of healing, but he did have a great interest in metaphysics, healing and the mind. Significantly influenced by Ralph Waldo Emerson, transcendentalism and the tenants of Christian Science, Holmes became a popular writer and lecturer, eventually publishing the *Science of Mind* that became the "fundamental text of Religious Science."[27]

Emma Hopkins, the founder of Divine Science, did not personally experience healing, but those who came under her teachings claimed they did. Hopkins believed the Holy Spirit was "God the Mother-Spirit," and that the emancipation of women would usher in the reign of this Mother Spirit.[28]

Phineas Quimby, a clockmaker from Portland, Maine is also considered one of the earliest proponents of New Thought. Quimby's teachings were picked up by father and son Julius and Horatio Dresser and prompted through lectures and eventually a book titled *The Quimby Manuscripts,* published in 1921. The Horatios are "considered the founders of New Thought as a named movement."[29]

Hanegraaff's research on Quimby is revealing of the foundations of the New Thought movement. Quimby came onto the New Age scene early in the 1800s, adopting the hypnotic practices of Charles Poyen, which became known as mesmerism. Early on, Quimby emerged as a mesmeric healer who claimed his healing abilities sprang from clairvoyant and telepathic abilities that enabled him to "see" a person's illness and promote it via the internal mesmeric fluid or vital force within them. Further, the revelation of the root of their illness caused their mind to bring healing to their body. This is in line with the "New Age belief which holds that we create our own reality, including our own illness or health."[30]

An early frontrunner in the New Age "healing and growth" movement, Quimby adopted practices that we see still in use today such as magnetized water as a prescription/medicine, the practice of aura reading, and the ability "to implant images of health directly into his patient's subconscious minds, from where they would materialize in the physical body by mediation of the psychic atmosphere."[31]

The core of the New Thought message was that individuals could "take responsibility" for their situation; it told them that the only reason why external circumstances seemed to have any power over them was because they believed that to be the case. The breakthrough to this realization was equivalent to a religious conversion.[32]

The New Thought movement paved the way for the Psychology and Religion Movement that emerged in the 1880s. It also prefigured the Human Potential movement of the 21st century,[33] which essentially ushered in the psychologization of religion and the sacralization of psychology that pervades Western culture today. Although New Thought theology claims the Christian Bible as its primary text, it is in fact a syncretistic blend of Christianity and New Age philosophy. In 1916, the International New Thought Alliance published the following as their statement of purpose: "To teach the Infinitude of the Supreme One; the Divinity of Man and his Infinite Possibilities through the creative power of constructive thinking and obedience to the voice of the indwelling Presence which is our source of Inspiration, Power, Health and Prosperity."[34]

The New Thought movement, perhaps more than any other group found within Western Esotericism, reflects the syncretistic nature of New Age. The book and teachings of the popular self-help genre, *The Message*, are based upon 19th century New Thought teaching.

American Transcendentalism

"Transcendentalism is an American literary, political, and philosophical movement of the early nineteenth century, centered on Ralph Waldo Emerson."[35] Henry David Thoreau and Ralph Waldo Emerson are two of the most well-known transcendentalists, along with less familiar names like Margaret Fuller, Theodore Parker and Bronson Alcott. Russell Goodman, in his article titled *Transcendentalism*, has this to say: "Stimulated by English and German Romanticism, the Biblical criticism of Herder and Schleiermacher, and the skepticism of Hume, the transcendentalists operated with the sense that a new era was at hand."[36]

The roots of American transcendentalism can be found among "the liberal New England Congregationalists" who split from orthodox Calvinism to become what we now call Unitarians. They discarded the trinity of God for the unity of God, believing that Jesus, although greater than humans was "inferior to God."[37]

William Ellery Channing, in his 1819 sermon "Unitarian Christianity," proposed "that human beings 'partake' of Divinity, and that they may achieve "a growing likeness to the Supreme Being."[38] Although

Unitarianism would grow and eventually take its place in the landscape of religion in America, it was not entirely embraced by the transcendentalists, who believed that there was "no empirical proof of religion that was satisfactory."[39] Their growing skepticism led to the idea that the Bible was not the divinely inspired word of God, but merely "a product of human history and culture," and "suggested that texts with equal authority could still be written."[40] Ralph Waldo Emerson went one step further when he said, "Why should we not have a poetry and philosophy of insight and not of tradition, and a religion by revelation to us, and not the history of theirs."[41] His 1838 graduation address to the Harvard Divinity School brought sharp criticism for his portrayal of the church as a monarchy that was injurious, and Jesus as "just one of the 'true race of prophets.'"[42]

The American Transcendentalist movement would enjoy a brief seventy-six years before fading from the American landscape, but it would leave behind a body of literature that would impact future authors such as Walt Whitman, Herman Melville, and Nathaniel Hawthorne.

Neopaganism

Current day Neopaganism, also known as Paganism, and often spelled Neo-Paganism, is a nature-based religious movement which emphasizes a reverence for nature while harkening back to ancient pagan religious traditions and rituals. It shares common characteristics but has many diverse forms. Neopaganism can be seen in modern day Wiccan practices and in Hellenic Polytheism.[43]

While Neopaganism is "not [considered] an organized religion," Neopagans do share many common beliefs. Neopagans engage in a variety of rituals or seasonal festivals and in practices that are "rooted" in "nature's divinity," such as astrology and divination. They honor gods and goddesses along with "ancestral and locational spirits" such as "deceased relatives."[44]

While some within the Neopagan movement would like to separate themselves from the New Age Movement, scholars such as Hanegraaff categorize it as part of the New Age Movement and yet a "clearly circumscribed subculture within that movement."[45]

Hanegraaff considers Wicca the "founding movement of modern witchcraft" and neopaganism as "fanning out" from Wicca.[46] Wicca is considered a religion and those who practice Wicca are called witches, although it is important to understand that not all witches practice Wicca. There are a wide variety of beliefs and religious systems that witches adhere to and Wicca is just one of them. Witchcraft itself, which is the practice of magic and the casting of spells, is considered a learned skill and does not have to be attached to any particular religious belief.

Wicca was founded in the 1950 in England by Gerald Gardner and has its roots in Celtic and Norse pagan religion.[47] It was brought to the U.S. in the 1960s by Raymond Buckland.[48] One prominent aspect of Wicca is its appeal to the feminist movement and women's spirituality, which gave rise to a spinoff of Wicca called the Goddess movement.[49] "Wiccan rituals and mythology are centered around the Goddess and her male partner, the Horned God. The polarity of male and female expressed by these divinities is basic to the Wiccan worldview."[50] For Wiccans, time is cyclical and reincarnation is part of that cycle. Wiccans are polytheistic, believing in many Gods, and pantheistic, believing that gods are part of nature.

Witchcraft itself has a long history. As early as 2000 B.C. there was mention of witchcraft in Babylon.[51] In the 3rd century AD, witches were burned alive in pre-Christian Rome.[52] In 1275, Hugues de Baniol confessed to "giving birth to a monster after intercourse with an evil spirit and to having nourished it with babies' flesh which she procured in her nocturnal expeditions."[53] She was burned to death in France. In 1647 the first witch was hanged in New England.[54] Some two hundred years later Gerald Gardner, founder of Wicca, was born in 1885.[55] In

1890 Aleister Crowley joined the Hermetic Order of the Golden Dawn, a magical order which began in England in the late 19th century, and which exerted significant influence on Western occultism in the 20th century.[56] Well-known Irish poet and author William Butler Yeats was also a member of the Golden Dawn.[57] In 1910, Crowley was initiated into the German Masonic order, Ordo Templi Orientis, and progressed through the degrees of the order, eventually being named the Grand Master for England and Ireland. Ordo Templi Orientis (OTO) was founded in the early 1900s and was based on a system of ritual sexual magic, the practice of which was supposed to reveal the key to understanding magic symbolism.[58] Witchcraft continued to flourish in Europe and North America. *The Rebirth of Witchcraft* was published in 1989, giving a first-hand account of the development and history of Wicca.[59]

Hellenic Polytheism is a form of Neo-paganism that attempts to restore the religious practices of the ancient Greeks with an emphasis on the worship of their deities or gods in exchange for favor and blessings.[60] Most Hellenic polytheists shy away from eclectic forms of ancient rituals in favor of authentic reconstruction of ancient practices. This puts them in opposition to Wiccans and other modern Neopagans. They have their own organization which ordains priests, each one dedicated to a specific god or goddess.[61]

Neopaganism has had a significant impact upon the New Age Movement, with its emergence as part of the counter-culture hippie movement in the 1960s to 1970s.

It is out of these occult roots that energy healing modalities Reiki and Therapeutic Touch emerged. Thinly disguised as "Christian" healing practices, they have gained surprising popularity in Western culture, due in no small part to the fact that the Church failed to understand or promote the practice of Christian healing.

Endnotes

¹Wouter J. Hanegraaff, *New Age Religion and Western Culture: Esotericism in the Mirror of Secular Thought* (Albany, New York: State University of New York Press, 1988), 386.

²Ibid.

³Ibid.

⁴Hanegraaff, *New Age Religion*, 393-394.

⁵Stewart Hawkins, Theosophy, The Religious Movements Homepage Project, 1998 and Ashcraft, Michael W. Modified 2005, (The original article was created by Steward Hawkins for Sociology 257, University of Virginia, Fall 1998. It was last modified by W. Michael Ashcraft, Truman State University, July 12, 2005.). http://web.archive.org/web/20060830023227/http://religiousmovements.lib.virginia.edu/nrms/theosophy.html (accessed January 31, 2013).

⁶Sarah M. Pike, *New Age and Neopagan Religions in America* (New York, NY: Columbia University Press, 2004), 64.

⁷*Encyclopedia Britannica Online*, s. v. "Alfred Richard Orage," http://www.britannica.com/EBchecked/topic/430735/Alfred-Richard-Orage (accessed January 31, 2013).

⁸James R. Lewis and J. Gordon Melton, *Perspectives on the New Age* (Albany, NY: SUNY Press, 1992), xi.

⁹1 John 2:22-23 Who is the liar? It is the man who denies that Jesus is the Christ. Such a man is the antichrist—he denies the Father and the Son. No one who denies the Son has the Father; whoever acknowledges the Son has the Father also. (NIV)

¹⁰R.T. Kendall, *Understanding Theology: The Means of Developing a Healthy Church in the 21st Century* (Scotland: Christian Focus Publishers, 1998), 370. Dr. Kendall had one of the highest GPA's of the doctoral graduates of The Southern Baptist Theological Seminary. He received a second doctorate from Oxford University in England and followed D. Martyn Lloyd Jones as pastor of the Westminster Chapel in London, where he ministered for over 20 years.

¹¹John T. Driscoll, "Theosophy," *The Catholic Encyclopedia*, Vol. 14, New York: Robert Appleton Company, 1912, http://www.newadvent.org/cathen/14626a.htm (accessed January 27, 2013).

¹²Ibid.

¹³Ibid.

[14] Helen Blavatsky, *EP Letters to friends and co-workers,* Collection, Trans with England, –M, 2002. – S. 249.

[15] Helen Blavatsky, *My Books*: Lucifer, Vol. VIII, NO. 45, May, 1891, 196.

[16] Helen Blavatsky, *The Secret Doctrine* (Theosophical Publ. Co, OCLC 61915001, 272–273 [Volume I], 1888), 272-273.

[17] Michael B. Wakoff, "Theosophy," *Routledge Encyclopedia of Philosophy*, 9 (New York: Routledge, 1998), 363–366.

[18] Wouter J. Hanegraaff, *New Age Religion,* 449. I have a power point regarding Hanegraaf's teaching .The slide presentation is available from the online bookstore at Global Awakening.com.

[19] Hanegraaff, *New Age Religion,* 439.

[20] Hanegraaff, *New Age Religion,* 449.

[21] J. Gordon Melton, et al, "Chronology of the New Age Movement," *New Age Encyclopedia*, 1990, Detroit: Gail Research, 1990. Taken from a four page section in the New Age Encyclopedia titled (xxxv-xxxviii), 458-461.

[22] "Christian Holidays," *Religion Facts*, February 8, 2007, [from "Updated:" on the left of the article, December 8, 2007] http://www.religionfacts.com/christianity/holidays.htm (accessed January 25, 2013).

[23] Ibid.

[24] Ibid.

[25] Ibid.

[26] "Christian Holidays," *Religion Facts.*

[27] Ibid.

[28] Ibid.

[29] Ibid.

[30] Hanegraaff, *New Age Religion,* 485-486.

[31] Ibid., 486.

[32] Ibid., 489.

[33] Ibid., 490.

[34] "Christian Holidays," *Religion Facts.*

[35] Russell Goodman, "Transcendentalism," *The Stanford Encyclopedia of Philosophy (Spring 2011 Edition)*, Edward N. Zalta (ed.), http://plato.stanford.edu/archives/spr2011/entries/transcendentalism/ (accessed January 25, 2013).

[36] Ibid.

[37] Ibid.

[38] Goodman, *Transcendentalism*.

[39] Ibid.

[40] Ibid.

[41] Ralph W. Emerson, *Nature*, 1836.

[42] Ibid.

[43] "Christian Holidays," *Religion Facts*.

[44] Ibid.

[45] Hanegraaff, *New Age Religion*, 79.

[46] Ibid., 85

[47] "Christian Holidays," *Religion Facts*.

[48] Hanegraaff, *New Age Religion*, 85.

[49] Ibid.

[50] Ibid.

[51] "Christian Holidays," *Religion Facts*.

[52] Ibid.

[53] Ibid.

[54] "Christian Holidays," *Religion Facts*.

[55] Ibid.

[56] Ibid.

[57] Ibid.

[58] Ibid.

[59] Ibid.

[60]Ibid.

[61]"Christian Holidays," *Religion Facts*.

CHAPTER FOUR
ENERGY HEALING MODALITIES: REIKI AND THERAPEUTIC TOUCH

Energy healing modalities such as Reiki and Therapeutic Touch have gained popularity within the emergent field of natural medicine and within traditional allopathic medicine, with degree programs and training offered throughout the United States and around the world. "Close to one hundred nursing colleges teach the practice, and tens of thousands of health care professionals have been trained in it. A survey in 2000-2001 found that of hospitals in the United States offering complementary and alternative medicine, almost half provided Therapeutic Touch as an inpatient service."[1] Registered nurse Sharon Fish, in her article *Therapeutic Touch,* wrote:

> Conservative estimates are that close to 100,000 nurses have been trained to perform the technique called Therapeutic Touch…
>
> Therapeutic Touch has been taught as a required or elective part of the curriculum in over 80 colleges and universities, with research-based and popular anecdotal articles abounding in nursing journals… Funding for Therapeutic Touch is readily available and much of it

is federal. Examples include a $200,000 grant by The Division of Nursing, U.S. Department of Health and Human Services to D'Youville Nursing Center in Buffalo, New York to train student nurses in the technique,[2] and a Department of Defense grant of $355,000 to a research team at the University of Alabama, Birmingham to study the effects of Therapeutic Touch on burn patients.

An Office of Alternative Medicine has also been established within the National Institutes of Health (NIH) to fund research on unconventional interventions. This attests to the popularity of Therapeutic Touch and related practices, such as Reiki, Reflexology, and Rolfing.[3]

"No licensing, professional standards, or formal regulation exists of the practice of Reiki."[4]

Many health insurance plans now cover the cost of treatment from Reiki and Therapeutic Touch, referring to them as "alternative medicine." Billboards and promotional literature from some hospitals in New England promote Reiki and Therapeutic Touch as "healing like Jesus heals," enabling these practices to gain acceptance among Christians.

An examination of the energy healing therapies Reiki and Therapeutic Touch reveals that they are not Christian in origin or in practice. Wouter Hanegraaff has this to say about New Age energy therapies: "Energy healing encompasses a broad range of therapeutic modalities, all of which focus on channeling healing energy into a client's body. The practitioner's role is to help bring energy fields into balance and improve the health and wellness of body, mind and spirit."[5]

Channeling refers to "the conviction of psychic mediums that they are able, under certain circumstances, to act as a channel for information from sources other than their normal selves. Most typically, these sources are identified as discarnate "entities" living on higher levels of being . . ."[6] There is trance channeling, automatic channeling, clairaudient channeling and open channeling.[7] "Channeling may be either intentional or spontaneous."[8] "Because it is widely believed in

New Age circles that channeling is a natural ability which is latent in everybody, the phenomenon of intentional channeling has resulted in the publication of do-it-yourself books with instructions for getting in touch with one's personal guide."[9] These personal guides are also referred to as "spirit guides."

Reiki

Reiki is defined as "a type of ancient healing that involves a balance of energy transfer and relaxation." Reiki Master Pamir Kiciman says that "Reiki energy is the same subtle energy that enlivens all of creation."[10] There are several different traditions of Reiki, some of Chinese origin. The Westernized version practiced most commonly in the United States is the Japanese tradition of Reiki. The website "Natural Healers," which is a clearing house for a variety of alternative therapy training schools, says this about Reiki: "Dating back to the 1800s, Reiki healing originated in Japan and is based on Buddhist and Hindu teachings. Today, you will find Reiki training available at a number of natural health schools in the United States."[11]

Reiki is pronounced "ray-key" and is a Japanese word that refers to the universal life force energy of a higher power. "Rei" in Japanese is loosely translated as "God" or a higher power. "Ki" is similar in thought to "chi" or "qi" in Chinese medicine and is translated from Japanese to mean "life force energy." There are also similarities in relation to Hindu "prana" and Christian "light." Reiki Master William Rand attempts to align Reiki with Christianity by promoting the teaching that "universal life energy" also means "God" as defined in Christianity, and in fact it is God in the form of the Holy Spirit.[12] This is incorrect. We will examine Christine doctrine more closely in Chapter 7.

Reiki, as defined by Reiki practitioners, is a hands-on energy healing practice in which the Reiki practitioner serves as an open channel for transmitting the "ki" into others. Reiki practitioners claim that they are able to channel the universal life energy through their hands and into the bodies of their clients. Once this energy enters the body it "knows" precisely where to go, enabling it to target places that need healing. At the same time that it is targeting, it is also activating natural energy found in the body to promote healing. Driven by unknown spiritual forces, which are often likened to God, this universal life energy, or Reiki energy, also unblocks and flushes toxins from the body according to Reiki teaching.

The story of the origin of Reiki is interesting, although the accuracy of many aspects of the story have proven false. The story was altered in order to "Americanize" Reiki so that it would be acceptable to the West, especially since it was introduced in Hawaii at the start of World War II and the bombing of Pearl Harbor by the Japanese. It was also Christianized in an effort to heighten its acceptance.

As the story goes, in 1865, a young Japanese Buddhist named Mikao Usui became a Christian and embarked on a quest to find the healing light of Christ. This quest sprang from the inquiries of his students at the Christian boys' school of which Usui was headmaster and chaplain. Records from the Reiki organization started by Usui indicated that he was in fact not a Christian, but a Buddhist who became a Buddhist monk later in life and upon his death was buried at a Buddhist temple.

The "altered" version of Usui's story continues with Usui studying at the University of Chicago and eventually receiving a Doctor of Theology degree. He did not, in fact, attend the University of Chicago or any other American university, nor did he receive a degree from an American university. Reiki Master William Rand is forthright in documenting these inaccuracies on his website.[13]

As the false narrative continues, Usui, frustrated at the cessationist theology of liberal Protestantism, eventually returned to Buddhism where he began an exhaustive study of its ancient texts in search of a secret healing path. His studies led to symbols found in Tibetan Buddhism written in Sanskrit, which form the basis for today's practice of Reiki.

In search of "divine" guidance, Usui went into retreat where he claims he experienced a visitation of light from the heavens that transmitted the meaning of the Sanskrit symbols to him. As a result of this experience, Usui received instant wisdom that we are to lay hands on one another in order to share the energy of love.

Usui also claimed that it was this mystical experience that formed the basis for Reiki, an original form of healing that he developed, when in fact what Usui called Reiki had been practiced for centuries in Asia. Those who knew Usui stated that as a young man he studied kiko, an ancient Japanese energy healing practice which relies on "ki" energy transmitted through the hands of a practitioner to heal. The words inscribed on Usui's Buddhist memorial tell us that he traveled in Europe and Asia studying medicine, psychology, religion and divination. He enrolled in Isyu Guo, a twenty-one-day training course sponsored by the Tendai Buddhist Temple located there.[14] The actual facts of Usui's life indicate that he aggrandized the healing art of Reiki from a variety of ancient metaphysical disciplines that formed the basis of his spiritual education.

Reiki training involves three levels or degrees, and is based in part on the three original Sanskrit symbols delineated by Usui. Reiki practitioners are taught that it is the use of these ancient symbols that allows them a temporary connection to unknown spiritual powers from which the Reiki energy flows. They receive their training in the form of attunements which are passed to them from Reiki masters. It is these attunements and the use of the ancient symbols that enables the Reiki practitioner.

It is surprising that the medical community has so willingly embraced Reiki since scientific research has been unable to prove its effectiveness. "A 2009 review in *The Journal of Alternative and Complementary Medicine* found that 'the serious methodological and reporting limitations of limited existing Reiki studies preclude a definitive conclusion of its effectiveness.'"[15]

Reiki has been identified with the divine healing known to Christians, with claims that it "heals like Jesus heals," when in fact this is not the case. In Christian healing, the healing power is at God's disposal. But for the Reiki practitioner, the healing power is at human disposal. Some Reiki proponents want to avoid this implication by arguing that it is not the Reiki practitioner personally that effects the healing, but the Reiki energy directed by the divine consciousness.[16] We will examine the issue of whose energy is at work in these various healing modalities in a later chapter.

For Christians, the access to divine healing is by prayer to Jesus Christ as Lord and Savior, while the essence of Reiki healing is not prayer but a technique that is passed down from the "Reiki Master" to the pupil. It is believed that this technique, once mastered, will reliably produce the anticipated results. Some practitioners attempt to Christianize Reiki by adding a prayer to Christ, but this does not affect the essential nature of Reiki. For these reasons, Reiki and other similar energy healing techniques cannot be identified with what Christians call healing by divine grace.

Another difference between what Christians recognize as healing by divine grace and Reiki therapy is evident in the basic terms used by Reiki proponents to describe what happens in Reiki therapy, particularly that of "universal life energy." Neither the Scriptures nor the Christian tradition as a whole speak of the natural world as based on "universal life energy" that is subject to manipulation by the natural human power of thought and will. In fact, this worldview has its origins in eastern religions and has a certain monist and pantheistic character. Distinctions among self, world and God tend to fall away. We have already seen that Reiki practitioners are unable to differentiate clearly between divine healing power and power that is at human disposal. This worldview was the propaganda of James Cameron's 2009 movie *Avatar*.[17] Reiki therapy finds little support in the findings of natural science, and no basis of support in Christian belief.

Therapeutic Touch

Therapeutic Touch is another alternative energy healing modality that has gained wide acceptance in modern medical practice. Like Reiki, Therapeutic Touch has been promoted by some as healing like Jesus heals in an effort to give it a thin veneer of acceptability among Christians.

According to Therapeutic Touch's own website, this energy healing modality originated at the Pumpkin Hollow Retreat Center (PHRC), "A spiritual retreat center of the Theosophical Society in the foothills of the Berkshires in New York State."[18] As you will recall from our discussion of Theosophy in Chapter 3 of this book, it is decidedly anti-Christian with roots deep in the occult. The website goes on to say, "In 1972, Dora [Kunz] and her longtime student and colleague Dolores Krieger, PhD, RN, developed Therapeutic Touch (TT). They developed a program for teaching the procedures and attitudes necessary for TT. Formal classes began at PHRC, where patients were referred by their physicians."[19] Sharon Fish, in her article titled *Therapeutic Touch* writes: "Therapeutic Touch was formally introduced to the nursing world in a 1975 article published in the *American Journal of Nursing (AJN)*, one of the most widely read journals for practicing nurses." The author was Delores Krieger, R.N., Ph.D., a professor at New York University (NYU).[20]

It is of particular note that Dora Kunz was at one time President of the Theosophical Society.[21] As a young woman, she was mentored by Charles Leadbeater, an influential author on the occult who rose through the ranks of the Theosophical Society and was instrumental in its spread to Australia.[22]

The actual practice of Therapeutic Touch does not involve the laying of hands but is achieved by placing the practitioner's hands near the patient in an attempt to detect and manipulate the person's energy fields, which is supposed to promote self-healing.

In April of 2011 the American Cancer Society published an article on their website about Therapeutic Touch, stating definitively that there is currently no available scientific evidence to support the claims made by practitioners and proponents of Therapeutic Touch who claim that it cures diseases, specifically cancer. The article cites irritability, restlessness, dizziness and nausea as some of the reported side effects, and warns cancer patients not to rely solely on Therapeutic Touch for treatment of cancer. They [The American Cancer Society] acknowledge that Therapeutic Touch is similar to the practice of Reiki, with both of these energy healing modalities channeling energy into the body as has been done in Asian cultures for centuries.

This same article presents statistics regarding training in Therapeutic Touch from a 2005 survey. Of the 1,400 hospitals that responded to the survey, 30% offered training in Therapeutic Touch, joining "more than a hundred" colleges and universities around the country and in Canada who train both health care professionals and nonprofessionals.[23]

In May of 2010, David Reed, Professor Emeritus and Research Professor at Wycliffe College, University of Toronto, Canada, presented a paper titled *Healing – In the Atonement or in the Fingers?* at a public lecture for the Synergy Institute for Leadership in Hong Kong. In this paper he looks at alternative energy healing modalities both from the perspective of theology and science. In his examination of Therapeutic Touch he references Dolores Krieger's book *Accepting Your Power to Heal* as the 'Bible' for Therapeutic Touch based upon the advice of friends who incorporate TT in their Christian healing ministries.[24] Reed writes:

> Her approach as set out in her book, *Accepting Your Power to Heal*, breathes the zeitgeist of the last 20th century, including ideas familiar in the New Age Movement. Its popularity is undoubtedly due in part to the yearning of our present culture.[25]

Reed goes on to point out how Krieger initially attempts to "build her theoretical framework on a scientific basis"[26] because she is conscious of the appeal of scientific validity to the Western mind. Once she has established what she feels is scientific validity she shifts to Eastern spirituality. Reed continues:

> She lays out her philosophy, a form of humanistic anthropology, in four premises which she believes are agreeable to both East and West: (1) human beings are an 'open energy system,' (2) human beings are anatomically 'bilaterally symmetrical,' (3) illness is the result of an 'imbalance' in a person's energy field, and (4) human beings have the capacity to 'transform and transcend' their life situation.

> The first is informed by the new science of quantum physics, the second and third are distinctively Eastern, and the fourth is a form of idealism familiar in both cultures. The benefits are attractive in our stress-related world: relaxation, pain reduction, hastening of the healing process, and relief of psychosomatic illness.[27]

> To summarize, Krieger seems to be stating that a scientific explanation of a human energy field based on quantum physics is what Eastern healers have practiced for millennia. Her confidence in human potential fits well with the Western field of humanistic psychology represented in theorists like Abraham Maslow. Yet she subtly moves into the realm of "spirituality," however undefined. This incorporation of spirituality into other disciplines such as psychology represents a recent trend in fields that in the past eschewed such topics.[28]

This synchronistic blend of science, Eastern mysticism, psychology and occult spirituality is a hallmark of the New Age Movement. The energy healing modalities that come out of the New Age Movement do not resemble Christian healing in any way.

Like its counterpart Reiki, Therapeutic Touch finds little support in the findings of natural science. The problematic nature of Kreiger's research methods ultimately yielded nothing of value to support her [Kreiger's] claims. Therapeutic Touch research in general has been so problematic as to be labeled fraudulent by the National Council Against Health Fraud.[29] Let's turn our attention now to an examination of Christian healing.

Endnotes

[1] Donald O'Mathuna and Walter L. Lairmore, *Alternative Medicine* (Grand Rapids: Zondervan, 2001, 2007).

[2] Sharon Fish, "Therapeutic Touch," Article ID: DN105, Christian Research Institute, CRI, http://www.equip.org/articles/therapeutic-touch/ (accessed January 25, 2013).

[3] Partap Khalsa, D.C. and John Killen, Jr., M.D., "Reiki: An Introduction," Pub. No. D315, National Center for Complementary and Alternative Medicine (NCCAM), http://nccam.nih.gov/health/reiki/introduction.htm#hed6 (accessed January 25, 2013).

[4] "Energy Healing Schools and Careers," *Natural Healers*, 1990-2013, http://www.naturalhealers.com/qa/energy.html (accessed January 25, 2013).

[5] Hanegraaff, *New Age Religion*, 27.

[6] Ibid., 28.

[7] Ibid.

[8] Ibid.

[9] Ibid.

[10] "Energy Healing Schools and Careers," *Natural Healers*.

[11] Ibid.

[12] William L. Rand, "Reiki: The Healing Touch, First and Second Degree Manual" (Expanded and Revised ed.), Reiki, (The International Center for Reiki Training.). http://www.reiki.org/FAQ/HistoryOfReiki.html (accessed January 25, 2013). (Mrs. Takata Speaks, The History of Reiki, CD and transcript (Southfield, MI: Vision Publications, 1979). Tadao Yamaguchi, Light on the Origins of Reiki (Twin Lakes, WI: Lotus Press, 2007), 66).

[13] Rand, "*Reiki.*"

[14] Shiomi Takai, "Searching the Roots of Reiki," *The Twilight Zone* (April 1986): 140–143. This article can be viewed on the web at http://www.pwpm.com/threshold/origins2.html. (Note that this Japanese magazine is no longer in business.)

[15] S. vanderVaart, V. Gijsen, S. Wildt, and G. Koren, (2009), "A Systematic Review of the Therapeutic Effects of Reiki." *The Journal of Alternative and Complementary Medicine* 15 (11): 1157–1169.

[16] Rand, *Reiki*. For a full explanation of Rand's attempts to Christianize Reiki go

to his site: http://www.christianreiki.org/ (I believe it is impossible to Christianize Reiki or Therapeutic Touch because their worldview is antithetical to the Christian worldview, the former being Pantheistic, and the latter being Theistic.)

[17]Avatar, Dir. James Cameron, Perf. Sam Worthington, Zoe Saldana, Stephen Lang, Movie, Twentieth Century Fox, 2009.

[18]Therapeutic Touch Defined, Pumpkin Hollow Farm, (2004), http://therapeutictouch.org/what_is_tt.html (accessed January 25, 2013).

[19]Ibid.

[20]Fish, *Therapeutic Touch*.

[21]Dora Van Gelder, (Gale Group, Inc. 5th Edition. ,1625), ISBN 0-8103-9489-8

[22]Ibid.

[23]American Cancer Society, *Therapeutic Touch*, April 2011, eb., http://www.cancer.org/treatment/trementandsideeffects/complementaryandalternativemedicine/manualhealingandphysicaltouch/therapeutic-touch (accessed January 25, 2013).

[24]David A. Reed, (2010) *Healing in the Atonement or the Fingers?* Synergy Institute for Leadership in Hong Kong.

[25]Ibid.

[26]Ibid.

[27]Ibid., 12.

[28]Ibid., 13.

[29]Fish, *Therapeutic Touch*.

CHAPTER FIVE

CHRISTIAN HEALING

Christian healing is best examined through the lens of the Christian worldview, because the two cannot in fact be separated. Christianity is theistic, which means that the Christian understanding of God is that He is a loving Father who is all powerful. He is the creator of all things and the source of all things. The Oxford Dictionary of the Christian Church defines theism as "the existence and continuance of the universe is owed to one Supreme Being, who is distinct from Creation."[1] James Sire in his book *The Universe Next Door* puts it this way:

> So the greatness of God is the central tenet of Christian theism. When a person recognizes this and consciously accepts and acts on it, this central conception is the rock, the transcendent reference point, that gives life meaning and makes the joys and sorrows of daily existence on planet earth significant moments in an unfolding drama in which one expects to participate forever, not always with sorrows but someday with joy alone. . . . Their [Christians] first act is toward God – a response of love, obedience and praise to the Lord of the Universe, their maker, sustainer and, through Jesus Christ, their redeemer and friend.[2]

God is also Trinitarian, that is, three divine yet distinct persons in one – Father, Son, and Holy Spirit. As the Father He is transcendent and immanent to His creation. As the Son He manifests himself as the "only-begotten Son" (John 1:14 NASB). He is God come in human form to live a human existence, to redeem us to God and to usher in God's kingdom on earth. The Son reveals God the Father to us. God the Father made the universe through the Son (Hebrews 1:2) and it is through the death, resurrection and ascension of the Son that we have been given eternal life (John 10:28).

The Holy Spirit is to be worshiped with the Father and the Son as the third person of the Trinity (2 Corinthians 13:14). He is co-equal, co-eternal, of the same essence as the Father and the Son.[3] He is the source of supernatural gifts (1 Corinthians 12:8-10). It is in the Holy Spirit that the immanence of God is most readily experienced in the lives of believers.

Let's look more closely at Jesus the Son, the Holy Spirit, and the Christian understanding of human personhood. Each are central to Christian healing.

The Christian understanding of Jesus is quite different from the New Age understanding of Jesus, and it is from this difference that more heresy has occurred than any other place in Christian theology. Heretical views have arisen in His relationship to His deity and to His humanity.

Jesus is the incarnation of the second person of the Trinity. He is not one of many "christs." He is not one of many masters. He is not one of many ways to salvation. He is "the way, the truth, and the life," and "No one can come to the Father except through [Jesus] me" (John 14:6 NLT). "Salvation is found in no one else, for there is no other name under heaven given to men by which we must be saved" (Acts 4:12).

The Holy Spirit is the source of special revelation that comes through preaching of the gospel, reading the Bible, or participating in the sacraments. "All Scripture is inspired by God and is profitable for teaching, for rebuking, for correcting, for training in righteousness, so that the man of God may be complete, equipped for every good work" (2 Timothy 3:16-17 HCSB).

Scripture also says, "First of all, you should know this: no prophecy of Scripture comes from one's own interpretation, because no prophecy ever came by the will of man; instead, moved by the Holy Spirit, men spoke from God" (2 Peter 1:21 HCSB).

The emphasis on the relationship between the Holy Spirit and receiving revelation is very important because both New Age religion and the Christian religion are based upon revelation. Neither is based solely upon human philosophical reasoning. Both have a basis of knowing rooted in experience, the experience of communications with spirits that are outside our normal human communications. For Christians there are not only angelic spirits and demonic spirits that can communicate to us, but the most important source of communication is from the Holy Spirit.

The Holy Spirit does not communicate approval for the immoral actions which characterize occult practices, such as sex outside of marriage as an act of worship. The Holy Spirit brings revelation from God that gives witness to Jesus as the Son of God come in the flesh for the salvation of all mankind.

The Holy Spirit also gives Christians the power to work signs and wonders within the constraints of a dependent relationship. Unlike New Age practices, which channel an impersonal energy, Christian healing goes beyond what can be done with the help of a "spirit." Christian healing is dependent on the leading of the Holy Spirit who brings word (revelation) from the Father and the Son, and power to do miracles in Jesus' name.

The understanding of human personhood is very different within the Christian and the New Age religions. Christians believe that we are not immortal souls, but that each person has a beginning and a soul that was created at conception. We do not experience reincarnation or transmigration of the soul. Our blessed hope and the final desire of our souls is the return of Christ to earth to consummate His kingdom, at which time we will be gathered to Him for all eternity.

The New Age view is that our souls are immortal and existed prior to our bodily existence and will survive death to be reincarnated. The reward in New Age religion, for all the pain and sorrow of repeated reincarnations is the loss of self-identity, loss of history, loss of relationships, loss of self-consciousness. We are simply assumed into the consciousness of the "One."

As we examine healing as it is manifested within Christianity, we see that more than any other major world religion, Christianity places the greatest emphasis upon healing. About one-fourth of the gospels deal in some way with the healing ministry of Jesus. We see this emphasis continuing in the book of Acts, which is the first recorded history of Christianity, and into the epistles, which include the ministry of healing as the primary display of a sign or wonder.

The basis for healing within Christianity is found in the New Covenant, the Atonement, and in the message of the Kingdom of God.

The New Covenant

Before the birth of Christ, mankind operated under the Old Covenant established at Mount Sinai when God gave the Israelites the Ten Commandments. These were physical laws to be obeyed. Obedience brought blessings from God and disobedience brought curses.

Jesus came to initiate the Kingdom of God, the Church, and the New Covenant. His life, death and resurrection delivered us from the Old Covenant's curse and redeemed us from the penalty of death under the Old Covenant laws. "For this reason Christ is the mediator of a new covenant, that those who are called may receive the promised eternal inheritance – now that He has died as a ransom to set them free from the sins committed under the first covenant" (Hebrews 9:15), and for the penalty for those sins, which, according to Deuteronomy 28 include sickness.

So what exactly is the New Covenant? Jon Mark Ruthven tells us in his forthcoming book *What's Wrong with Protestant Theology* that the New Covenant is the goal of the Bible[4] and that the content of the New Covenant is "the experience of the prophetic Spirit – hearing God's voice."[5] It was at the Last Supper (Luke 22:14-23) that Jesus instituted the New Covenant as an ongoing relationship between God and Christian believers. Jesus understood that His death on the cross, His blood shed on the cross, would once and for all time fulfill the requirements of the Old Covenant, creating the New Covenant between God and His people. Some 600 years before the birth of Christ, the prophet Jeremiah spoke of this New Covenant:

> 'This is the covenant I will make with the house of Israel after that time,' declares the Lord. 'I will put my law in their minds and write it on their hearts. I will be their God and they will be my people.'
>
> Jeremiah 31:33

As Ruthven points out, [Divine] revelation from God leads to fellowship with God.[6] It is out of this fellowship with God, this relationship with God, this hearing His voice and being led by His Spirit, that Christian healing flows. The power of God to heal is present for us in His Divine revelation that flows from the New Covenant mediated by Jesus Christ.

New Age energy healing modalities have none of the rich covenant history found in Christianity that is grounded in the revelation and power of God to heal in Jesus Christ. They are instead a series of amalgamations of occult theologies and practices and their healing energy comes from occult sources over which they have no control.

The Atonement

The atoning death of Jesus on the cross provides the basis for our faith and it is where we find our healing. On the cross Jesus bore both our pain and sickness and our sins and iniquities.

The great suffering servant passages found in Isaiah 52:13 through Isaiah 53:12 capture the essence of the meaning of the cross. Isaiah 53:3 says, "He was despised and rejected by men, a man of sorrows, and familiar with suffering." The English "sorrows" translates the original biblical Hebrew, *mak'ob* which means "mental pain, anguish." Likewise the Hebrew translation of suffering is *kholi,* which means "sickness, disease." So Jesus bore our sicknesses and diseases and our mental anguish and pain on the cross.[7]

In Isaiah 53:4 it says, "Surely he took up our infirmities and carried our sorrows, yet we considered him stricken by God, smitten by him, and afflicted." The Hebrew for "took up" is *nasah* and means "to lift up from, carry away." So, He [Jesus] lifted up our sickness and disease and carried away our pains.[8]

In Isaiah 53 verse 12, "For he bore the sin of many," we find the Hebrew *nasah* again – to lift up from and carry away, but in this instance He is not lifting our sickness and disease but our sin.[9]

The Message of the Kingdom of God

The kingdom of God is both now and not yet. It is a literal kingdom to come that will be ruled over by Christ. It is the fulfillment of the Lord's Prayer found in Matthew 6:9-10:

> 'Our Father in heaven, hallowed be your name, your kingdom come, your will be done, on earth as it is in heaven.'

When Jesus returns in glory He will establish His kingdom once and for all. But, just as this kingdom is yet to come, it is also here now. God's authority and power arrived on the earth with Jesus who brought the kingdom with Him. And He left it here for each believer. The power of His kingdom is present in believers today, both individual believers and the Church.

With Jesus, the kingdom of God has come near, not as a place, but as the reign of God whose sovereign rule and authority were made manifest in Jesus. When Jesus taught His disciples to pray "Your kingdom come, your will be done, on earth as it is in heaven" (Matthew 6:10) He wasn't just telling them to pray for a physical kingdom to come, but also to pray for the will of God to be done on the earth. When the will of God is done on the earth, His rule and reign is established and His kingdom comes.

In the New Testament Jesus proclaims the message of the Kingdom of God over and over again, constantly and consistently, in words and in deeds. The "deeds" He used to proclaim His Kingdom were the healings and miracles, which were physical signs of the presence of God's reign on earth. Jesus tells us this in Matthew 11:4-5 when He says, "Go back and report to John what you hear and see: the blind receive sight, the lame walk, those who have leprosy are cured, the deaf hear, the dead are raised, and the good news is preached to the poor."

The atonement, the New Covenant and the Kingdom of God came together on the cross. Jesus' atoning death ushered out the Old Covenant and sealed the New Covenant so that God's kingdom could establish its rule over sin.

The ministry of healing flourished in the early church, yet much of what the Church has been experiencing in the last 1,700 years falls short of the experiences of the early Church. We have allowed doctrine to relegate the ministry of healing to the stuff of history in most mainline Christian denominations.

But things are changing. The Church is returning to the kind of Christianity that Jesus died to establish. We are now witnessing a mighty move of God within the Church that is bringing a revival of healing and a rediscovery of the message of the Kingdom of God. We are experiencing His presence and His power in miracles, signs and wonders and the gifts of the Holy Spirit.

The 20th century saw more healings and miracles than were seen in the first three centuries of the Church. The blind see, the deaf hear, the lame walk and the dead are being raised. In fact, in the last decade of the 20th century and the first seven years of the 21st century the Church has seen more people raised from the dead than any other time in its history. I have personally witnessed blind eyes opening, deaf ears hearing, the lame walking, and I personally know people who have seen the dead raised. I will share some of these amazing miracles of God later in this book.

Contrast this to testimonies of New Age healing. There are reports that people feel calmer or more peaceful after receiving Reiki or Therapeutic Touch, but the power of God to heal is not manifested through these New Age healing modalities or any other New Age practice. Does the reason for this lie in the source of the energy involved? I believe it does.

Endnotes

[1] "Theism," Oxford Dictionary of the Christian Church, Third ed., 2005.

[2] James Sire, The Universe Next Door, Fifth ed. (Downers Grove, IL: InterVarsity Press, 2009), 46. (Taken from The Universe Next Door, 5th Edition by James W. Sire. Copyright(c) 2009 by James W. Sire. Used by permission of InterVarsity Press, PO Box 1400, Downers Grove, IL 60515. www.ivpress.com)

[3] The Apostles Creed, the Nicene Creed and the Chalcedon Creeds.

[4] Jon Mark Ruthven, What's Wrong with Protestant Theology? Traditions vs. Biblical Emphasis (Tulsa, OK: Word & Spirit Press, 2013).

[5] Ibid.

[6] Ibid.

[7] Randy Clark, Healing is in the Atonement; The Power of the Lord's Supper (Mechanicsburg, PA: Global Awakening. 2012).

[8] Ibid.

[9] Ibid.

CHAPTER SIX
WHOSE ENERGY IS IT?

Both Reiki and Therapeutic Touch use the word "energy" in their vocabulary, and confusion abounds as to the source of this energy. To better understand the differences in the meaning of "energy" as it is used in energy healing modalities and Christian healing, it is important to first understand the differences between theistic and pantheistic theology.

We have already defined theism as a "philosophical system which accepts a transcendent and personal God who not only created but also preserves and governs the world, the contingency of which does not exclude miracles and the exercise of human freedom."[1] Further, we know that Theism purports that this one God is distinct from His creation. Theism is monotheistic. The word monotheism is derived from the Greek *monos* which means "only" and *theos* which means "god."

In contrast, the *Oxford Dictionary of the Christian Church* defines pantheism as "the belief that god and the universe are identical," with no division between the creator and His creation.[2] Pantheism is polytheistic, meaning that it believes in multiple gods. The *Catholic Encyclopedia* summarizes pantheistic doctrine as follows:

> Reality is a unitary being; individual things have no absolute independence - they have existence in the All-One, the *ens realissimum et et perfectissimum* of which they are the more or less independent members; The All-One manifests itself to us, so far as it has any manifestations, in the two sides of reality - nature and history; The universal interaction that goes on in the physical world is the showing forth of the inner aesthetic teleological necessity with which the All-One unfolds his essential being in a multitude of harmonious modifications, a cosmos of concrete ideas (monads, entelechies). This internal necessity is at the same time absolute freedom or self-realization.[3]

The *Catholic Encyclopedia* goes on to say,

> It has often been claimed that pantheism by teaching us to see God in everything gives us an exalted idea of His wisdom, goodness, and power, while it imparts to the visible world a deeper meaning. In point of fact, however, it makes void the attributes which belong essentially to the Divine nature. For the pantheist God is not a personal Being. He is not an intelligent Cause of the world, designing, creating and governing it in accordance with the free determination of His wisdom. . . He attains to self-consciousness only through a process of evolution (Hegel). But this very process implies that God is not from eternity perfect: He is forever changing, advancing from one degree of perfection to another, and helpless to determine in what direction the advance shall take place.[4]

The concept from a New Age perspective is that we are divine; we are gods. The Christian understanding of this truth is that we are not divine. We are created by God and distinct from Him. With this basic understanding of theism and pantheism, let us now look at "energy" as it is defined in Reiki and Therapeutic Touch.

Reiki Energy

Reiki, as we defined it previously, is pronounced "ray-key," and is a Japanese word that refers to the universal life force energy of a higher power. Rei" in Japanese is loosely translated as "God" or a higher power. "Ki" is similar in thought to "chi" or "qi" in Chinese medicine and is translated from Japanese to mean "life force energy." There are also similarities in relation to Hindu "prana" and Christian "light."

Reiki practitioners claim that it is a higher intelligence (wisdom) that guides the energy used in Reiki, and that this higher power is found in everything in the universe, in both animate and inanimate objects. It creates, it guides and it "helps" us. They claim that the "Ki" energy in Reiki flows through every living thing and is obtained from the air and sunlight, food and rest. According to Reiki, "Ki" energy levels can ebb and flow, causing disruptions in health when the energy is low, rather than the functional condition of the physical organs and tissues being the primary determinant of our overall health. Several other Asian civilizations have a term in their vocabulary for "Ki." In India it is known as "prana," and in China "Chi." The 19th century scientist Carl Reichenbach dubbed this energy force the "odic force," a term which has found its way into our 21st century media culture. Reiki practitioners say that Reiki energy possesses an intelligence of its own, flowing where it is needed in the client, and creating the healing conditions necessary for the individual's needs.

Therapeutic Touch Energy

According to the American Cancer Society, which does not promote the use of Therapeutic Touch, practitioners and proponents of Therapeutic Touch believe that pain and illness are caused by imbalances in the body's energy fields, and that trained practitioners can detect these imbalances and bring healing by unblocking and balancing the body's energy.[5]

Much like Reiki, Therapeutic Touch maintains that there is a healing life energy that can be transferred from practitioner to recipient through invisible pathways in the body. Sharon Fish, R.N. of the Christian Research Institute says:

> Long-time practitioners of Therapeutic Touch maintain that the human body is simply a localized expression of a universal energy system. The body is built up and maintained by nourishment but penetrated and kept alive by an energy called *prana* (a Sanskrit word meaning "vital force") that flows through and is transformed by energy centers in the body called *chakras* (Sanskrit for 'circle' or 'wheel'). Healthy people have an overabundance of *prana*; ill people have a deficit. A person with an overabundance of *prana* can deliberately, with conscious intent, transfer this energy to a patient. The energy flow surrounding the ill person can be perceived, that is, intuitively assessed and directed through the hands of a healer in the absence of any physical contact.[6]

Theistic or Pantheistic Energy

At this point we can ask if this healing "energy" we are speaking about is God as understood from a Christian theistic perspective, or nature (god) as understood from a pantheistic perspective.

Healing within the context of Christianity is dependent upon a relationship with a personal God. Christian theology responds to God with humility and praise as it acknowledges God's reign through Jesus and the Holy Spirit. Christianity believes the "Spirit" [Holy Spirit] is personal and not to be confused with "life force" or "magnetic energy."[7]

The New Age healer is independent and learns how to control, manipulate, and channel an impersonal energy (god). Krieger calls this "a humanization of energy."[8] New Age theology neither reveres nor adores God, but instead considers each person god. The New Age, with its re-sacralization of the universe, implies that "energy" is a vital fundamental reality of the universe and worthy of worship in and of itself because of its sacred nature.[9]

The Bible speaks frequently and clearly about Satan's desires to deceive believers and non-believers alike. This is part of the battle that rages as the two kingdoms, the kingdom of God and the kingdom of this world, war with one another. The Apostle Paul, when writing to the church in Thessalonica says, "The coming of the lawless one will be in accordance with the work of Satan displayed in all kinds of counterfeit miracles, signs and wonders, and in every sort of evil that deceives those who are perishing" (2 Thessalonians 2:9-10).

Dr. Reed says, "We are called to discern between the sorcerer's toolbox and Christian rites and symbols of healing, between self-interest and healing as a sign of divine love and compassion and instrument of the Reign of God."[10]

God reveals himself when He acts in miraculous ways. When Satan performs counterfeit miracles, he is unable to reveal the nature of God. Instead he reveals himself in lying signs and wonders.

Reiki Master and Episcopal Priest Ruth Mayeux Allen, in her dissertation *Pneumatology: The Spirit of Reiki*, maintains that "Reiki healing energy seems to guide itself and seems to contain a higher intelligence or power."[11] Although I think Allen would like us to believe that this "healing energy" is the Holy Spirit, I do not see that she has successfully proven that the spirit of Reiki is the Holy Spirit. I believe her attempts to connect the spirit of Reiki to the Holy Spirit fail for many theological reasons, which I have outlined in chapter 7 of this book.

Allen claims that "nowhere in the Bible can one find an occurrence of Satan healing someone." Either Ms. Allen does not know the Bible or she is making an untrue statement. There are many healing deities and gods in the ancient Near East that scripture categorically classifies as demons. For example, in the Bible in 2 Kings 1:2-3, we find Baal-Zebub the healing deity of Ekron. In this particular story King Ahaziah of Israel seeks Baal-Zebub's counsel when he is injured.

In Christianity Baal-Zebub is known as Satan. When the Pharisees accuse Jesus of driving out demons by the power of Baal-Zebub (Mark 3:22) they were attempting to align His power to heal with evil.

Sharon Fish, in the section titled "Supernatural Concerns" in her article *Therapeutic Touch* says:

> At the very heart of the controversy over Therapeutic Touch lies a question about the true (not merely perceived or constructed) nature of reality and the true nature of any energy involved in its practice. Not all energy forces are scientifically verifiable and explainable by the natural laws of this world for a primary reason: they are not all *of* this world. According to biblical theism, there is such a thing as supernatural, metaphysical reality and supernatural forces are at work *in* the world — forces of good (of God) and forces of evil (of Satan).
>
> It is not safe for anyone to assume that the energy Therapeutic Touch enthusiasts claim to be channeling is a force of good or godly power. In fact, it seems safe to conclude that it is not, as it is clearly associated with world views that are in opposition to Christianity and practices explicitly forbidden in Scripture. And those practices are clearly associated with attempts to make contact with spiritual (not truly scientific) forces and manipulate them in various ways.[12]

Theologian Dr. Gary Greig has this to say about Reiki and the energy involved in Reiki:

> The healing ministry of Jesus, the apostles, and the Church is focused on the multi-dimensional sin-war, as the Kingdom of God invades the kingdom of darkness in part by casting out demons. Reiki healing does not cast out demons; it makes no mention of casting out, evicting, or exorcising demons which is a central part of scripture's two kingdom healing theology and practice.[13]

I do believe that the Bible confirms that there is a universal life force energy which the scripture calls "the breath of life," however outside of Christ it is low-grade power at best, and defiled and demonic at worst. All power, even the power of Satan and demons, is given by God. (Revelation 13:7, 15) This universal life force is not to be confused with the Holy Spirit although scripture shows it was created by the Holy Spirit.[14]

The Committee on Doctrine of the United States Conference of Catholic Bishops in its guidelines for evaluating Reiki says:

> The Church recognizes two kinds of healing; healing by divine grace and healing that utilizes the powers of nature. As for the first, we can point to the ministry of Christ, who performed many physical healings and who commissioned his disciples to carry on that work. In fidelity to this commission, from the time of the Apostles the Church has interceded on behalf of the sick through the invocation of the name of the Lord Jesus, asking for healing through the power of the Holy Spirit, whether in the form of sacramental laying on of hands and anointing with oil or of simple prayers for healing, which often include an appeal to the saints for their aid. As for the second, the Church has never considered a plea for divine healing, which comes as a gift from God, to exclude recourse to natural means of healing through the practice of medicine.[15]

Dr. Gareth Leyshon, St. John's Seminary, Wonersh, England, in his paper titled *A Catholic Critique of the Healing Art of Reiki* has this to say about Reiki energy:

> In any case, techniques to manipulate ki would constitute the sin of 'tempting God' except where clearly founded in revelation from the Triune God. If ki were established to be spiritual, but did not meet the above conditions for being due to the Triune God, then its source must be the human soul (psychic energy) or evil spirits. The invocation of evil spirits is both sinful and potentially dangerous, and clearly forbidden to Christians.[16]

Dr. Leyshon goes on to say that the Catholic Catechism "forbids as 'gravely contrary to the virtue of religion' all 'attempts to tame occult powers, so as to place them at one's service and have a supernatural power over others – even if this were for the sake of restoring their health.'"[17] In his pastoral response to Reiki he writes:

> Evidence from those exercising the ministry of deliverance and exorcism indicates that deliberate and informed choices to resort to non-Christian spiritual powers can result in the form of demonic attack known as obsession or infestation, and that uninformed exposure to such powers (as might be the case with a person who receives Reiki having been assured that it is a simple form of 'healing touch') can result in the lesser form of demonic irritation known as oppression. Anecdotal evidence indicates that involvement in Reiki has led to Christians needing deliverance, although the nature of the cases makes it difficult to publish evidence. It must be stressed, however, that demonic attack is vulnerability, not a certainty, for those who have exposed themselves in these ways... Christians are committed to turn to no spiritual source other than the Triune God, who has not revealed Reiki as a means of harnessing His power.[18]

The Holy Spirit is the source of God's power to heal. As the apostle Paul said, "To this end I labor, struggling with all his energy, which so powerfully works in me" (Colossians 1:29).

God's energy is much stronger than that experienced through Shamans, witches, warlocks, spiritualist, and other New Age channelers. One of His gifts is the discerning of spirits – a gift that enables a person to determine whether or not the spirit being dealt with is good or bad in reference to the human spirit, and in reference to non-human spirits, whether or not it is godly or evil.

Are we seeing lying signs and wonders in New Age with its occult roots and deceptive practices? Let's examine the evidence.

Endnotes

[1] "theism" Oxford Dictionary of the Christian Church.com, *Oxford Dictionary of the Christian Church*, 2009, Web (accessed January 25, 2013).

[2] Ibid.

[3] Edward Pace, "Pantheism," *The Catholic Encyclopedia*, Vol. 11, New York: Robert Appleton Company, 1911, http://www.newadvent.org/cathen/11447b.htm (accessed January 25, 2013).

[4] Ibid.

[5] American Cancer Society, *Therapeutic Touch*, April 2011, eb. http://www.cancer.org/treatment/treatmentsandsideeffects/complementaryandalternativemedicine/manualhealingandphysicaltouch/therapeutic-touch (accessed January 25, 2013).

[6] Fish, *Therapeutic Touch*.

[7] Reed, 2010.

[8] Ibid., 18.

[9] Ibid., 17.

[10] Ibid.

[11] Allen, 2009.

[12] Fish, *Therapeutic Touch*.

[13] I have a power point presentation with 15 slides that outline my teachings on this subject. I have compiled this material in conjunction with theologian Dr. Gary Greig. It is also part of my doctoral dissertation which is soon to be published. This presentation is available from the online bookstore at Global Awakening.com At the bookstore type into the search window, *15 Christian Doctrines Rejected by Reiki* which will take you to the downloadable power points where they may be purchased.

[14] Ibid.

[15] <u>Guidelines for Evaluating Reiki as an Alternative Therapy</u>, Committee on Doctrine, United States Conference of Catholic Bishops, by the Most Rev. William E. Lori, chairman, 2009.

[16] Dr. Gareth Leyshon, Catholic Critique of the Healing Art of Reiki, <u>Abstract</u>: *The Complementary Therapy {A Catholic Critique of the Healing Art of Reiki}*, United States Conference of Catholic Bishops, 2009.

[17] Ibid.

[18] Ibid.

CHAPTER SEVEN
EXAMINING THE EVIDENCE

I believe one of the reasons New Age practices and beliefs have been able to deceive so many is because the Church has failed to adequately educate believers in Christian doctrine. This chapter is by no means an exhaustive study on Christian doctrine. It is a brief overview of some of the doctrines of Christianity that are pertinent to our study of healing, both within Christianity and in New Age.

In chapter 5 we examined Christian healing through the lens of the Christian worldview and came to understand that it's impossible to separate the two. We examined the Christian understanding of Jesus versus the New Age rejection of Jesus. We explored the source of revelation as coming from the Holy Spirit or from spirit guides. And we looked at the doctrine of the human being, or human personhood, as understood through the lens of Christian doctrine versus the New Age worldview. We found stark differences in each instance, differences that amount to a rejection of Christian doctrine by New Age.

There are several other Christian doctrines that have been emphatically rejected by the New Age worldview of which Reiki and Therapeutic Touch are a part. We will briefly examine each one.

The Doctrine of Creation versus Eternal Matter/Pantheism and the Doctrine of God's Nature (personal) versus Non-personal

The doctrine of creation as understood from within the Christian worldview demonstrates the position of man. Genesis 1:26-27 says:

> Then God said, 'Let us make man, in our image, in our likeness, and let them rule over the fish of the sea and the birds of the air, over the livestock, over all the earth, and over all the creatures that move along the ground. So God created man in his own image, in the image of God he created him.

We were created in the likeness and image of God but not as God, who made man from the dust of the earth and infused him with His divine nature: "the Lord God formed the man from the dust of the ground and breathed into his nostrils the breath of life, and the man became a living being" (Genesis 2:7).

In contrast, the New Age belief in the origin of life and of the universe purports that life - including the universe, matter and all things - were not created by God, but instead these things are god. They were not created but emerged out of a power found in the eternal universal life force. This is pantheism - everything is one.

Panentheism is distinguished from pantheism in that pantheism sees god as the whole, whereas panentheism sees that the whole is in god. While pantheism asserts that god and the universe are coextensive, panentheism claims that god is greater than the universe and that the universe is contained within god. Hinduism is highly characterized by both panentheism and pantheism.[1]

New Agers treasure the teachings of pantheism because it means that they also are gods/goddesses. This teaching, however, loses much of its appeal when it is revealed that the rat rummaging through the garbage is also God according to pantheism. If pantheism is true then it means that even garbage is God. It means that a slug is God. It means that a worm in an apple is God. It means that maggots are God.

Another problem with pantheism is that God must ultimately be understood as impersonal and not as a personal being. If this is true, it means that the impersonal must be greater than (or at least the same value as) the personal. But even New Agers find it very difficult to live as if this is true. They tend to view animals as having more value than an impersonal rock. They tend to view their families as having more value than a plant. When New Agers live as if the personal is of more value than the impersonal, they act as if the teachings of the Bible, and not pantheism, are true. The God of the Bible is a personal God distinct from His creation.

The Bible issues strong warnings to those who confuse God with His creation: "Although they claimed to be wise, they became fools and exchanged the glory of the immortal God for images made to look like mortal man and birds and animals and reptiles" (Romans 1:22-23).

Both our experience of reality and the teachings of the Bible contradict the New Age belief that we are God. The Bible teaches that while humanity was created in the image of God, mankind is not and never will be God (Genesis 1:26-27). Isaiah 43:10 says, "'You are my witnesses,' declares the Lord, 'and my servant whom I have chosen, so that you may know and believe me and understand that I am he. Before me no god was formed, nor will there be one after Me.'"

The Doctrine of the Human Being (Personhood) versus 'Same' as God

Many New Agers teach the death of God - that our sensation of existing as finite creatures is an illusion and that humanity has forgotten that it is divine. As a result, people need to become enlightened about their true divinity in order to experientially become one with the All.

New Agers believe that exercises intended to transform consciousness can help one attain enlightenment. Techniques such as Buddhist meditation, past-life regression, soul travel, and channeling spiritual guides may help one achieve enlightenment. Many of the consciousness-altering techniques used by New Agers are occultic and forbidden by the Bible. God condemns the use of divination, sorcery, witchcraft, magical spells, mediums, and spiritualists (Deuteronomy 18:9-12).[2]

The New Age gospel calls not for faith in Jesus Christ, but rather for a shift in consciousness. New Agers believe this change of consciousness will only be achieved when we no longer see God as separate from us and no longer see ourselves as separate from each other. This is "death of a sense of self" as understood from a Christian perspective.

Christianity understands that humanity's problem is sin, not ignorance of divinity. While human beings have been created in the image of God, they are not divine (see Genesis. 1:26-27). The Bible teaches, "all have sinned and fall short of the glory of God" (Romans. 3:23). The only solution to the human predicament is faith in Jesus Christ as Lord and Savior.

The Doctrine of Time (linear) versus Circular (reincarnation)

Wouter Hanegraaff details the syncretistic blend of evolution and reincarnation that formed the basis for Theosophy, which strongly influenced Therapeutic Touch: "The whole conceptual structure of progressive 'reincarnation' (actually spiritual progress by learning from experience during many lives in this *and* other worlds), which would be adopted by modern theosophy, and ultimately by the New Age Movement, already existed by the end of the 18th century.[3] New Age thinkers, Blavatsky in particular, merged the concepts of reincarnation and evolution. No longer were these religious or philosophical concepts, but in order to legitimize them for emergent Western thinking, they were elevated to the realm of science. Traditional theism was supplanted by occult theology. No longer was God the creator. Now we were all "creators." Physical evolution was a "law of nature," not the work of God, and the concept of spiritual evolution garnered from reincarnation was morphed into a natural force. Now humans could progress to higher and higher levels of spiritual existence, not only in the universe, but in other universes.

In progressive reincarnation we die and then we are reborn as a baby and live another life. Then we will die again and are reborn again, starting the process all over. These cycles of birth, life, and death are necessary in order to lose the illusion of separateness from the All, the One. We progress toward this Oneness by acquiring positive karma.

Karma is the fruit of our life and actions that are carried by the soul to its next life. Positive karma advances us toward realizing unity with the "All." Negative karma prolongs the time needed to realize this unity. In traditional Hinduism, negative karma can cause us to come back as a lower life form.

Blavatsky did not retain the possibility of coming back in a lower life form, since evolution theory was always progressive, never regressive. Neither did Blavatsky embrace the Hindu belief that there is a hell that Hindus could experience between cycles of reincarnation. She took only what fit with evolution from Hinduism and rejected what didn't fit with evolution. She went to the East to build a system that gave her theosophical system more legitimacy than its roots in the New Thought idealism of her time period in 19th century New England.

The Judeo-Christian perspective of history is a linear one in which all of humankind is moving through time from a specific created beginning (Creation) to a restorative end (second coming of Christ). This movement of humanity through time is non-repetitive and is directed by God.[4]

The Doctrine of the Resurrection versus Reincarnation

The Bible denies the possibility of reincarnation: "Just as man is destined to die once, and after that to face judgment . . ." (Hebrews 9:27). Since people will experience only one physical death, reincarnation cannot be true.

The Bible teaches resurrection, not reincarnation. Jesus declared, "I tell you the truth, a time is coming and has now come when the dead will hear the voice of the Son of God and those who hear will live" (John 5:25).

Reincarnation is a form of works salvation. The Bible rejects salvation through works (of any kind) as impossible. Romans 11:6 says, "And if by grace, then it is no longer by works; if it were, grace would no longer be grace." Likewise Ephesians 2:8-9 stresses that salvation from sin and its external consequences is a gift that God gives freely. Sin does not result in reincarnation but in death: "For the wages of sin is death, but the gift of God is eternal life in Christ Jesus our Lord" (Romans 6:23).

The Doctrine of Sin versus Sin and Evil are only Illusions

New Agers believe that since all is One, there is no difference between good and evil, or right and wrong, and therefore there is no such thing as evil. Morality becomes relative. Some New Agers even assert that evil comes from God. This is the understanding of Hinduism as well, with its worship of a god of destruction that is part of its polytheistic view of gods. This god is both the goddess Kali, the destroyer, and the god Shiva, the god of destruction. This understanding of God makes it impossible to declare the affirmation of Christianity, "God is good – all the time." Unlike Hinduism, New Age religion has no god or goddess of destruction. For New Age religion there is no evil.

While New Agers may try to explain evil by denying its reality, in order to deny the existence of evil they must also deny the validity of goodness. They not only deny the Bible, which condemns certain actions as wrong, but also deny their own consciences.

The belief that there is no difference between right and wrong is illogical because it contradicts itself. Its adherents claim it is right to believe there is no right or wrong. But if there is no right or wrong, then how can it be right to believe that there is no right or wrong?

Both the Bible and our life experiences support the Christian teaching that there is a distinction between good and evil, right and wrong. Also, the Bible clearly indicates that God is not the source of evil: "When tempted, no one should say, "God is tempting me." For God cannot be tempted by evil, nor does he tempt anyone" (James 1:13).

The Doctrine of Salvation versus the Unity with the 'One'

For the New Ager there is no such thing as sin and therefore there is no need to be saved. Instead they continually aspire to higher levels of consciousness until they at some point experience salvation, which flows from the realization of our 'oneness' with the impersonal life force of the universe. Some New Agers even believe that the salvation of humanity will happen when all people converge in the experience of our 'oneness' with god and each other until this convergence reaches a critical mass, at which time all will achieve salvation. This understanding of salvation finds no agreement with the Christian understanding of salvation.

The Biblical understanding of salvation is that it is available through Jesus the Christ, and Jesus Christ alone: "Jesus answered, 'I am the way and the truth and the life. No one comes to the Father except through me'" (John 14:6). In order to understand the Biblical concept of salvation we must first accept the reality of sin. It is our sin that separates us from God, necessitating our salvation.

The Doctrine of Jesus' Incarnation as Historical versus Non-historical; Separate the Man Jesus from the Christ Spirit; Jesus' Lordship as the Way versus the 'Way Show-er'

New Agers believe that there have been many "christs" - Confucius, Mohammed, and Buddha, in addition to Jesus. These "christs" are considered avatars. Avatar is a Hindu term which means "descent" in Sanskrit. "In Hinduism, an avatar is a deliberate descent of a deity to earth."[5] New Agers consider Jesus a reincarnated avatar sent to earth for the purpose of giving spiritual revelation. He is one "way show-er" among many "way show-ers."

In contrast, the doctrine of Christ's incarnation is the center of the message of the Gospel. His incarnation defines every area of Christian theology. Jesus is God come in the flesh, fully God yet fully human, and it is through His incarnation that God's true identity is revealed to the world.

It was at the incarnation that the "Word" became flesh. When we look at the incarnation of Christ in a linear, historical fashion, we see Christ as the living Word at the moment of creation, as told by the apostle John:

> In the beginning was the Word, and the Word was with God, and the Word was God. He was with God in the beginning. (John 1:1)

> Through him all things were made; without him nothing was made that has been made. In him was life and that life was the light of men. The light shines in the darkness, but the darkness has not understood it. (John 1:3-5)

> The Word became flesh and made his dwelling among us. We have seen his glory, the glory of the One and Only who came from the Father, full of grace and truth. (John 1:14)

Jesus, God come in the flesh, was not an afterthought, but the cornerstone of God's plan from before the beginning of time and for all eternity. Outside of the incarnate Christ we would not have a personal relationship with God. Without the incarnate Christ there would be no atoning death, reconciling humanity in its personal sins to a holy God. It is through the incarnation of Christ that God becomes personal.

When New Agers use the term "christ" to refer to a divine consciousness or spirit, they give it a meaning not found in the Bible. Christ is a Greek term that means "anointed one." The New Testament uses the term to designate Jesus as the promised Messiah of the Old Testament. Jesus warned His followers to be on guard against false teachers who would proclaim false christs (Matt. 24:24-25). The New Age view of the Christ Consciousness is one of these false christs. The Jesus of the Bible is unique. He is God's one and only Son (John 3:16). For Christians, Jesus is the way, not merely a "way show-er."

The Doctrine of the Second Coming as Reality versus 'Not a Reality'

New Agers believe the universe is evolving and that a new age of enlightenment and transformation is coming. They believe that our world is about to undergo a transformation to a higher level, and that this change will be brought about by a shift in human consciousness toward New Age paradigms.

There are parallels between the New Age expectation of a coming New Age and the Christian expectation of the consummation of this age and the coming of the "age to come." Both have views that are, on the one hand, dependent upon an apocalyptic event occurring at a time of historical crisis. This viewpoint almost always has reference to a messianic deliverer/savior. For the New Age it is unknown who this will be, but for the Christian it is the return of Jesus Christ.

From a biblical standpoint, we understand that a new world is coming. But it will not come about as a leap to a higher level, but through the second coming of Jesus Christ. God, in His own time and in His own way, will bring the world to its appropriate end, leading to a renewed earth

with the nature of paradise, where no natural evil occurs. According to
His promise, Jesus Christ will return personally and visibly in glory to the
earth; the dead will be raised; and Christ will judge all men in righteousness (1 Thessalonians 4:14-18). The ungodly will face destruction and the
righteous will dwell forever in heaven with the Lord (Matthew 7:13; John
17:12; Romans 9:22; Galatians 6:8; Philippians 3:19; 2 Thessalonians
1:9, 2:3; 2 Peter 2:3, 3:7, 12, 16; Revelation 17:8,11). It is interesting that
the viewpoint from the book of Revelation is that Heaven comes down
to earth; that God comes to earth in the symbolism of the heavenly New
Jerusalem, coming to the renewed perfected earth (Rev. 3:12; Rev. 21:2).

The Doctrine of Justice (Grace) versus Karma

To consider the doctrine of justice (grace) from a Christian perspective
versus the New Age doctrine of Karma, it is important to examine Blavatsky's interpretation of Karma. She essentially reinterpreted Karma to suit
her emerging theology. Discarding the original concepts of Karma as understood from the Buddhist and Hindu perspectives, she morphed it into a
scientific causal law of cause and effect in an effort to negate the possibility of
a personal God. To Blavatsky, there was no hand of providence, only karmic
law. The grace of God is not necessary because all are equal – we are all gods,
able to determine our own destiny as we return again and again, hopefully
on higher and higher spiritual planes.

The Christian understanding of grace is far superior to the concept of
Karma, especially as it is found in New Age thinking. For Christians, grace is
the unmerited favor of God. It is His mercy and compassion; an undeserved
blessing and a free gift. God's loving mercy toward mankind is synonymous
with God's gift of undeserved salvation in Jesus Christ. "For God so loved
the world that He gave his one and only Son, that whoever believes in him
shall not perish but have eternal life" (John 3:16). Grace is also understood
in terms of divine enablement, divine empowering with the power or energy

of God. Perhaps the best way to describe grace is in terms of *generous empowerment*. With this term, the traditional emphasis of generous would be connected to the stronger New Testament emphasis on *empowering*.

The writer of Hebrews says, "Let us then approach the throne of grace with confidence, so that we may receive mercy and find grace to help us in our time of need" (Hebrews 4:16). It is through Christ that we are able to approach this throne of grace, finding ourselves worthy to receive God's mercy and God's empowerment. Karma offers no such grace, neither as unmerited forgiveness or divine enablement. This divine energy is not a part of human potential, but is dependent upon the presence of God coming into the human body and situation.

When Christians pray for healing, it is by the grace of God in Jesus that healing comes. When Reiki or Therapeutic Touch is employed for healing, the practitioner is not seeking the grace of God to heal, but an energy force within themselves and others than is independent of God. There is a big difference between focusing on energy that comes from within a person (human energy), coupled with another energy that is independent of God, versus receiving by the grace of God healing in Jesus.

The Doctrine of Impartation ('Comes to Us') versus 'Is within Us'

The power of impartation comes to us as a supernatural gift from God, as we receive divine grace to be able to do in the natural what humanly can't be done. It comes by faith and is rooted in Jesus' death on the cross and the complete work of the cross. Jesus died not only to give the gift of salvation and eternal life, but also to give the power of signs and wonders, and healings and miracles, which reveal the loving kindness and generous nature of God.

The New Age understanding is that "power" to heal is within each of us, and in order to be able to use this power we need to learn how to access it and channel it to others.

I would like to end our brief examination of Christian doctrine as compared to New Age beliefs with this thought from James Sire, author of *The Universe Next Door*.

> To accept Christian theism only as an intellectual construct is not to accept it fully. There is a deeply personal dimension involved with grasping and living within this worldview, for it involves acknowledging our own individual dependence on God as his creatures, our own individual rebellion against God and our own individual reliance on God for restoration to fellowship with him. And it means accepting Christ as both our Liberator from bondage and Lord of our future... To be a Christian theist is not just to have an intellectual worldview; it is to be personally committed to the infinite-personal Lord of the universe. And it leads to an examined life that is well worth living.[6]

I believe with all my heart that Christ is our liberator from bondage and the Lord of our future. I live daily with the reality of His presence as I travel the world bringing the message of His power to heal and save. I see this mighty power of God manifest in miracles, signs and wonders over and over again. I know that God heals today because I see it happening all around me, and because I have personally experienced His healing power in my own body.

Endnotes

[1] Panentheism, *Encyclopedia of Philosophy*, ed. Paul Edwards (New York: Macmillan and Free Press, 1967), 34.

[2] "New Age Movement – Overview – 4Truth.NET," *4Truth.Net World Religions*, New Age, N.p., n.d. Web, http://www.4truth.net/fourtruthpbworld.aspx?pageid=8589952991 (accessed January 28, 2013).

[3] Wouter J. Hanegraaff, *New Age Religion and Western Culture: Esotericism in the Mirror of Secular Thought* (Albany, New York: State University of New York Press, 1988), 479-480.

[4] David Noebel, *Understanding the Times: The Collision of Today's Competing Worldviews* (Rev. 2nd ed), (Summit Press, 2006).

[5] Christopher Partridge, *Introduction to World Religions* (Minneapolis: Fortress Press, 2005), 148.

[6] James Sire, *The Universe Next Door,* Fifth Edition 2009 (InterVarsity Press, Downers Grove, Illinois), 285-286. (Taken from *The Universe Next Door*, 5th Edition by James W. Sire. Copyright(c) 2009 by James W. Sire. Used by permission of InterVarsity Press, PO Box 1400, Downers Grove, IL 60515. www.ivpress.com).

CHAPTER EIGHT
GOD HEALS TODAY

My own ministry of healing came out of the Jesus Movement and out of my own personal healing. I was a child of the 1960s and 1970s. God's revival burned across America during those years and sparked a flame in my heart that is still burning today. Much of my interest in the ministry of healing grew out of my own experiences of being miraculously healed.

Many of you have already heard my story of healing or read about it in one of my other books. If that's the case, you can skip this section if you like. I'm including it here because I feel it is important for those of you who haven't heard it yet. It is foundational for everything that I have done since, and has been my anchor through the years as the storms of religion and doubt have tried to derail me.

My miracle healing, like the scores of miracle healings that I have been privileged to see over the years, gives witness to the reality that God's gifts of healing and working of miracles are for the Church today. These healings give witness to the greatest source of power in the universe, the healing energy of God in the power of His Holy Spirit through Jesus Christ. God's ministry of healing has not ended and I am living proof.

My story begins in 1970. I was a senior at McLeansboro Township High School in southern Illinois. The late sixties and early seventies were not an easy time to be a young man in the U.S. There was a great deal of turmoil over the Vietnam War. Lots of drugs were beginning to appear, not just in the large cities, but in small towns across America, as thousands of young Vietnam veterans came home from the war and brought the drug culture with them.

I committed my life to Jesus Christ at the age of sixteen and had a powerful and dramatic experience of conversion. But by the age of eighteen I had become the prodigal son. I was involved in drugs and had adopted a culture of dishonor towards my elders and my parents. I was a hypocrite when it came to my Christian faith, but I wasn't a happy hypocrite. I missed the presence and peace of God that I had known growing up. Longing for that peace and presence again, I recommitted my life to Jesus on October 8, 1970, hoping to make a break from sin and rebellious behavior. I began trying to be faithful to God once again, and to walk with integrity. I wanted to live authentically.

The following Thursday I was driving home from college with my two best friends, Joe and George, and Joe's sister Marge, when a friend tried to pass me, lost control of his car and slammed into us, knocking my car off the road. I hit a concrete culvert, flipped end-over-end a few times, almost broke a telephone pole in half, and ended upside down in a ditch.

Somewhere in all that Joe was thrown through the windshield. He died of a broken neck. George wasn't hurt, but Marge was seriously injured, and I was too. I had multiple fractures in the face, three crushed areas the size of quarters in the hairline of my forehead, a fractured jaw, broken ribs, paralysis of my digestive system and twenty percent compression of the mid-spine vertebrae. The doctors told me I would be in the hospital for a long time; anywhere from seven weeks to three months.

There was concern initially, when I arrived by ambulance, that I could become a paraplegic if my spinal cord swelled, and if I moved the wrong way. I was in a semi-coma for the first few days, receiving 50 mg. of Demerol® every three hours, and was scheduled to be moved to a much larger hospital where they could better deal with the paralysis of my digestive system.

My pastor came to pray for me several times. My youth group met the night before I was to be transferred to Barnes Hospital in St. Louis. They prayed and by the next morning my digestive system was working properly. As a result I was not transferred.

That same morning one of the three specialists assigned to my care came into my room to set my broken jaw, but he couldn't set it because it had already been healed.

A few days later I woke up and the severe pain in my spine was gone. I had a strong impression to sit up in bed, even though I hadn't raised my head off the bed in over two weeks. I hadn't even been allowed to use a pillow. Well aware of the risk of permanent paralysis if I moved my back, I decided that I was going to obey this inner impression because I believed God was healing me. I got up and walked and after that the nurses couldn't keep me in bed. I kept telling the nurses that Jesus had healed me, and that I wanted to go home.

Within two weeks of the accident I had been healed of a broken jaw, paralysis of my digestive track, and severe pain in the spine. The doctors kept me in the hospital for another week and made me wear a brace. When they discharged me they told me to go home and go to bed. I went home, but I had no intention of going to bed. Instead I went to church and gave my testimony of God's healing.

As a result of my testimony a revival broke out four nights later, on Sunday evening. It lasted for forty-nine straight nights. The church experienced over two-hundred and fifty conversions, almost all of them young people in their teens or twenties.

Out of that revival, eleven young people were called into ministry. The oldest one was twenty-three. Raised in an alcoholic home, he had become one of the biggest drug pushers in the county. At one point in his life he had tried to commit suicide and ended up in a mental institute. He was gloriously saved and instantly delivered from his drug addiction and healed of Post-Traumatic Stress Disorder (PTSD) caused by his experiences in Vietnam, as well as the physical problems caused by drugs and Agent Orange.

I was the second of the eleven young men called into ministry. I remember the night well. It was November 20, 1970. I was eighteen years old. As a result of my own healing and the revival that ensured, my understanding of God changed and so did my expectations regarding healing. I realized that healing wasn't reserved for the saintly or for God's favorites, but was for everyone, even a recently backslidden sinner like me.

Fast forward thirty-nine years to the next miraculous healing to take place in my life. I was sitting on the floor at home in Pennsylvania, in the middle of a meeting. When I tried to get up, I found myself in terrible pain. Not since my car accident had I felt such pain. I couldn't move without severe pain.

The next day I was hosting a conference. Pushing through the pain, when I tried to stand up to introduce the first speaker, I couldn't get up. Two men had to carry me from the building.

I went to my chiropractor but he couldn't help me. After a barrage of tests it was determined that the bottom curve in my spine was totally gone, causing my disks to slip easily and pinch the nerves in my leg. I had three herniated disks, two pinched nerves, and two kinds of arthritis in my back. I couldn't walk without crutches. I wasn't supposed to sit. All I could do was lay on a pallet on the floor. After two epidural shots in the spine that didn't help, my only option left was spinal surgery.

Friends with strong healing gifts prayed for me but to no avail. My own prayers for healing weren't answered. I was disabled at that point, but God healed me again and in a most unexpected way.

Our oldest son Josh was living in Japan at the time and when he heard about my condition he called on Skype and prayed for me. I was stunned by the authority and anointing that was on him. The 24/7 pain, constant and unrelenting for weeks, suddenly left me. I was partially healed. I had no pain unless I tried to put weight on my foot. If I lifted my foot the pain stopped. I still had to walk with crutches, but the healing of the constant 24/7 pain for which I was taking Percocet and two other prescriptions was such a relief.

I stopped taking pain medication and started living again, but my healing wasn't complete. My leg still hurt when I walked. In fact the leg was so painful that I could only walk with crutches. I couldn't put any weight on the leg and it was extremely difficult to go up and down stairs.

This went on for about three weeks, and then I woke up one morning, got out of bed and the pain in my leg was gone. I had been healed during the night but I didn't fully understand what had happened until that afternoon when I read an email from a friend in Louisiana, Ray Smith. Ray told me that during the night he had a vision in which he saw me with Jesus. In the vision Jesus pointed to my back and told Ray to pray for me. He even showed Ray exactly where the problem was on my back. Ray saw my clothes, skin, and muscles disappear, allowing him to see my spine and nerves. The Lord showed him in the vision which nerves were pinched and which vertebrae had been damaged. The Lord told him to push the inner material of the vertebrae back in. This vision was so real that Ray sent me an email that night; I didn't open it until the following afternoon. I had been healed several hours before I received the email, making the possibility of the healing being due to the placebo effect impossible. Jesus healed me again and made me whole and I continue to thank Him every day. I had been told by the physical therapist that I had "classic traveler's back" from taking many international flights, and that I should never fly again. In the four years following my healing I flew over 600,000 miles.[1]

The ministry of healing that God has led me into and sustained for the last forty-three years flowed out of these two personal healings. It was slow going at first. I saw a few healings trickle through my church in the early years of ministering healing, but it wasn't until 1984, when I invited a team from the Vineyard Christian Fellowship to come and teach, that the floodgates opened. God showed up with that Vineyard team and a powerful outpouring of the Holy Spirit ensued. I received an impartation from the speaker when the Holy Spirit came upon me. The power was so strong that all my joints ached the next day as a result of the energy that ran through my body that night.

Five years later I received another impartation of the Holy Spirit that was so strong I feared it might kill me. The power was so strong it was painful. Four years later I received another impartation that resulted in a major outpouring of the Holy Spirit in my local church. This led to a speaking engagement at the denominational regional meeting where a major outpouring of the Spirit for impartation happened to almost every person present. This was October 1993.

Word of this powerful outpouring spread, and in January 1994 I was invited to speak at John Arnott's Airport Vineyard Christian Fellowship in Toronto, Canada. The initial invitation was to speak for four nights, but God had other plans. He poured out His Spirit with such power and might that four nights became twelve and a half years! People came from all over the world, six nights a week. The Toronto Blessing became the longest protracted revival meeting in the history of America.

In the years since Toronto there has been extraordinary increase in my ministry. The following January 1995 was a major breakthrough in healing. That month I saw more healings than in the preceding twenty-four years combined. Today I am seeing extraordinary things happen, some of which are totally incomprehensible to me. The in-breaking of the Kingdom of God is pushing back the kingdom of the devil with powerful miracles, signs and wonders that bring the Gospel alive to a hungry world. This mighty in-break of the Kingdom of God is not only happening in my own ministry, but in other ministries around the globe. You can read more about this global revival in my books *There is More* and *Changed in a Moment*.[2]

Endnotes

[1] This story of healing is told in: *There Is More; The Essential Guide to Healing; Lighting Fires.* They are available from the online bookstore at globalawakening.com or through Amazon or on Kindle.

[2] These books are available from the online bookstore at globalawakening.com.

CONCLUSION:

As I mentioned earlier, I have personally witnessed blind eyes opening, deaf ears hearing, and the lame walking. I have met the family members of people who were raised from the dead. I have seen with my own eyes the gospel of Jesus Christ as found in the Scriptures. I can give personal witness that the power of God to heal is for the Church today. The following stories are but a few of the hundreds and hundreds of healings I have seen take place in the years I have been ministering. We, the Church, are not powerless.

For many years now I have been taking teams all over the world to minister healing. On one of my international ministry trips, a seventeen year old woman was healed of deafness in both ears; a young man blind in one eye received his sight, a twelve year old girl walked out of a wheelchair which she had been in for about a month due to injuries from an accident. A pastor was healed of kidney stones one hour after prayer. Another young man in his twenties received a creative miracle for his knees. Let me tell you more about some of these people and how they were healed.

In the fall of 2012, I took a team of people, mostly lay people, who are not in full-time ministry, to Fortaleza, Brazil. During one of the worship services one of our team members gave a word of knowledge for a left ear. There was a young woman there, seventeen years old. She had been totally deaf from birth. This young woman was seated in a position so as not to be able to see our team, who were lined up at the front of the church to give words of knowledge. She began to touch her hand to her left ear several times, looked at her mother, and gave a gesture that she could hear. Her left ear had opened! A few seconds later another word of knowledge was given by another person on our team. Again, this young woman began hitting her right ear, and again the ear opened. For the first time in her life she could hear from both ears!

During the same church service there was a young man who had been born blind in one eye. The optic nerve was not connected to the back of his eye. He had become successful in business, and had returned to the doctors to ask if there was anything else they could do to restore his sight. Money was no object. The doctors told him, "Only God could cause the eye to see." It was medically impossible to restore sight to his eye. He received prayer from one of the members of our ministry team and was healed! The sight in his blind eye was restored.

A young girl of about twelve years of age came in a wheelchair to one of the church services in Fortaleza with her mother. About a month earlier she had been hit by a motorcycle while crossing the street in front of the church. Among her other injuries, her Achilles tendon had been damaged and she could no longer walk. She had also suffered a head injury which was causing double vision. During prayer she received healing for her tendon and the double vision. The large gash on her head, where her skull had cracked open from the impact, was also healed. It closed up and only a small scar was visible. She got out of her wheelchair and was able to walk again. When she gave her testimony we learned the rest of the story.

She was with her mother, in front of the church, crossing the street when a motorcycle hit her. The impact threw her many feet and caused her head to hit the curb. Her mother immediately ran to her side and saw that her daughter's head had cracked open and that her child was dead. She began to pray for her daughter. Someone called an ambulance. When the ambulance arrived the paramedic told the mother it was too late for prayer; her daughter was dead. This mother continued to pray, asking God for a miracle.

Fifteen minutes went by and she continued her prayers despite the paramedic's pleas. He kept telling her, "You have to let her go, she is dead. Your prayers won't help now." Despite his words, this mother called her cell group leader, who came to the scene of the accident and began to pray with her friend. Now the paramedic had two women praying for the resurrection of the girl. Frustrated, he finally told the women he was going to have to take the child's body to the morgue. At that point the two women commanded the child's spirit to come back into her body; she gasped for breath and was restored to life. She had been dead for approximately 30 minutes. This child was raised from the dead, her lameness healed and her vision restored to normal.

During this same mission trip, in October of 2012, we were in a church in Uberlandia, Brazil. We learned that there was an older woman from this church who was at home, close to death. She had visible tumors all over her body. So close to death was she that she had been instructed to say her last remarks to her family. In the absence of a priest, those with her prayed for her soul and blessed her; a Protestant "last rites" of sorts.

Three people from our larger team went to pray for her. When they arrived they were shocked at how close to death she was. Dr. David Zarisky, a retired radiologist, told me later that he was embarrassed by his own shock at her appearance. He simply prayed for her peace in death. The team made the decision to pray also for her healing and then left. About an hour later they received a telephone call that the woman had been healed. Her tumors had disappeared and she was up and out of her "death bed."

During this three week ministry trip in Brazil we also learned of another person who had been raised from the dead, an infant. This had happened about six years prior, in 2006. I was in Brazil at the time, at a church service with our team. A young mother, distraught, came to the service with a picture of her infant daughter. The baby had been declared brain dead and life support was about to be disconnected. She asked me to pray for her daughter, but she didn't tell me at the time that the baby was brain dead. Shortly after the prayer the baby came back to life. I did not know at the time that the baby had been brought back to life.

Fast forward six years, to our Fall 2012 mission trip to Brazil. This baby was now six years old. She had something wrong with her leg which required her to wear a brace. She had walked her whole life with a brace, but she had a great desire to walk without it. Her mother brought her to one of the services and the little girl began to walk without the brace. Her lameness was healed. We brought her up on the stage and she began running around the stage. We had trouble keeping up with her! It was at that point that her mother shared the rest of the story with us – that this was the infant in the picture that I had prayed for six years earlier, the infant that had been declared brain dead by her doctors.

There were several hundred people healed on this trip to Brazil in the Fall of 2012, however, it would be wrong to think that these types of healings only happen in certain places. These types of healings and miracles are happening all over the world. I am aware of 450 people who have been raised from the dead in Mozambique. I have met the family members of some of them. These resurrections occurred through the ministry of my friends and fellow apostolic leaders of the Revival Alliance, Rolland and Heidi Baker, and the leaders they are training and raising up. These resurrections, along with the thousands of other healings that have taken place in Mozambique, have resulted in over one million people coming to faith in Jesus. Two provinces that were entirely Muslim have now been recognized by the Mozambican government as Christian provinces.

These miracles of resurrection have encouraged me to believe for the healing of other serious conditions affecting the brain like Parkinson's, Multiple Sclerosis, strokes, and Cerebral Palsy. I did not see these types of healings in my own ministry until after I learned about the miraculous resurrections of the dead going on in other parts of the world. Since that time I have seen several healed of Parkinson's, Multiple Sclerosis and strokes. I am still contending to see healing of those with Cerebral Palsy.

In the last few months alone we have seen many people healed in the United States. In December 2012, in Illinois, and again in January 2013, in California, we saw two veterans healed of Post-Traumatic Stress Disorder. One had been a career soldier and a master sergeant with several deployments into war zones. The other had such severe PTSD that he could not be the man, husband, and father he wanted to be. Both received prayer from the director of the Global School of Supernatural Ministry, Mike Hutchings, and both were completely healed. The night sweats, the inordinate fear, the horrific night terrors and dreams, and the anxiety all left following a few minutes of prayer. In each case there were also other physical problems that were rooted in the trauma of their soul. The physical problems were healed when the emotional PTSD was healed.

In January 2013, I was ministering at a Baptist Church in Abilene, Texas with Jamie Galloway. Jamie is very gifted in the prophetic and had been ministering prophetically during the service. Among those in attendance was a man who was suffering from partial paralysis of the bottom half of his body as the result of an accident. He had lost bladder sensation and could not feel the bottoms of his feet, which made it difficult to walk. This man had come to the service with his heart hardened towards the prophetic and healing from a lifetime of sitting under cessationist teaching. He was healed during the service. In tears he shared how he could now feel bladder sensations and he could feel the bottoms of his feet. He was able to walk up and down the steps in the church normally rather than one step at a time. Apologizing to Jamie, he asked forgiveness for his hardness of heart. As a result of his own healing he was able to renounce the cessationist teachings that had separated him from the truth of the gospel of Jesus and to understand that the gifts of prophecy and healing are still for today.

I pray that you are as amazed by these stories of healing as I am. I pray that these testimonies to the power of God to heal will encourage you and stir your faith, and stir a desire in your heart to seek healing for yourself and those around you. And I pray that some of you will be so encouraged by these testimonies that you will respond to the promptings of the Holy Spirit and pursue the ministry of Christian healing.

When it became obvious to me that we, the Church, have failed to provide opportunities for you, the body of Christ, to learn about healing, and have failed to offer training in healing and the gifts of Spirit, both in the local church and in our seminaries and Bible colleges, I felt strongly that it was time to change that dynamic. To that end I have created an online certification program called the Christian Healing Certification Program (CHCP).

Through CHCP students will gain a strong understanding of the principles of Christian healing and the doctrinal basis for healing. They will receive practical, hands-on experience that will give them confidence in their ability to be led by the Spirit in the ministry of healing. Upon completion of the program, students will be certified to take the ministry of Christian healing into hospitals, clinics, churches, the workplace, and anywhere there are those in need of healing.

I believe that once those certified in Christian healing take their place in today's modern medical practice, alongside allopathic medicine and

New Age energy healing modalities, the results will speak for themselves. I believe that we will see that God's power to heal is much stronger than anything found in the New Age Movement. No longer will New Age energy healing modalities be the only "certified" choice for those of you seeking healing or training for healing.

I present this book not as a judgment but as an invitation; an invitation to find the power to heal and the power to move in the supernatural realm of spiritual gifts by returning to Jesus and learning how to heal as Jesus healed. Reiki and Therapeutic Touch market their systems as "teaching people to minister like Jesus," but in reality offer a very different model. The worldview and belief system of these New Age energy healing modalities are strongly opposed to the beliefs and claims of Jesus, and deny almost all the basic doctrines of Christianity. They do not teach how to minister as Jesus did, and they do not heal as Jesus healed. Their systems are not built upon the worldview of Jesus, but a worldview that contradicts Jesus' worldview of the relationship between the spiritual and the material, between God and people.

If you are a practitioner of one of the New Age energy healing modalities, I invite you to consider the information presented in this book and then decide whether you want to continue with occult practices or truly practice healing as Jesus healed. If you choose to follow Jesus and heal as He healed, you will become open to the Holy Spirit, the greatest source of spiritual power in the universe. You will truly be able to minister as Jesus did, because you will be empowered and enabled by *His* source and *His* Father, made available to Him by the Holy Spirit.

I realize those of you reading this book approach the issues presented here from many different angles. Some of you are practitioners of one or more of the New Age energy healing modalities. Others of you have received treatment from a New Age practitioner. Some of you are Christians and some are not. Some of you are Christians who are practicing Reiki and

Therapeutic Touch and other New Age healing modalities. And there are those of you who are just curious readers. Wherever you fall on this spectrum, the message is the same: New Age energy healing modalities are deeply rooted in the occult and should be avoided. The occult has nothing good to offer anyone. Christian healing is rooted in the Christian faith and everything it offers is good.

You are now armed with information and the choice is yours. I invite you to stay away from the occult. If you are in need of healing or want to embrace the practice of healing, then embrace Christian healing, because everything it offers is good. The power of God found in Christian healing is stronger than any other power known to man.

Some two thousand years ago the early Christian church saw God's power to heal:

> The apostles performed many miraculous signs and wonders among the people. (Acts 5:12)

> As a result, people brought the sick into the streets and laid them on beds and mats so that at least Peter's shadow might fall on some of them as he passed by. Crowds gathered also from the towns around Jerusalem, bringing their sick and those tormented by evil spirits, and all of them were healed. (Acts 5:15-16)

This same power of God to heal that is recorded in the book of Acts is still available today: ". . . open your eyes and see – how good God is. Blessed are you who run to him" (Psalm 34:8, The Message).

CONCLUSION

BIBLIOGRAPHY

Allen, Ruth Mayeux. "Pneumatology: The Spirit of Reiki." Master's thesis, School of Theology of the University of the South in Sewanee, TN, 2009.

American Cancer Society. *Therapeutic Touch*. (April 2011). eb. (accessed January 25, 2013). http://www.cancer.org/treatment/treatmentsandsideeffects/complementaryandalternativemedicine/manualhealingandphysicaltouch/therapeutic-touch

Blavatsky, Helen. *Blavatsky EP Letters to friends and co-workers*. Collection. Trans with England. –M, 2002. – S.249.

------, *My Books*: Lucifer, Vol. VIII, NO. 45, May, 1891, 241-247.

------, *The Secret Doctrine*, (Theosophical Publ. Co, OCLC 61915001, 272–273 [Volume I], 1888), 38.

Clark, Randy. *Healing is in the Atonement; The Power of the Lord's Supper*. Mechanicsburg, PA: Global Awakening, 2012.

DeArteaga, 1992. Hyatt, 1996. Ruthven, *On the Cessation of the Charismata: The Protestant Polemic on Postbiblical Miracles*. 1993. Ruthven, *What's Wrong With Protestant Theology?* 2013. Clark, *School of Healing and Impartation: Deliverance, Disbelief, and Deception Workbook:* 2009. Workbook 2011.

Driscoll, John T. "Theosophy." *The Catholic Encyclopedia*. Vol. 14. New York:

Robert Appleton Company, 1912. http://www.newadvent.org/cathen/14626a.html

Fish, Sharon. *Therapeutic Touch.* Article ID: DN105. Christian Research Institute. CRI. http://www.equip.org/articles/therapeutic-touch/ (accessed January 25, 2013).

Goodman, Russell. *Transcendentalism. The Stanford Encyclopedia of Philosophy.* Spring 2011 Edition, Edward N. Zalta (ed.). http://plato.stanford.edu/archives/spr2011/entries/transcendentalism/ (accessed January 25, 2013).

Hanegraaff, Wouter J. *New Age Religion and Western Culture: Esotericism in the Mirror of Secular Thought.* Albany, New York: State University of New York Press, 1988.

Hawkins, Stewart. *Theosophy.* The Religious Movements Homepage Project. 1998 and Ashcraft, Michael W. Modified 2005. (paper, University of Virginia, Charlottesville, Virginia, Sociology 257, 1998.) (Modified by W. Michael Ashcraft, Truman State University, July 12, 2005.)

http://web.archive.org/web/20060830023227/http://religiousmovements.lib.virginia.edu/nrms/theosophy.html (accessed January 25, 2013).

Khalsa, Partap, D.C., and John Killen, Jr., M.D. *Reiki: An Introduction.* Pub. No. D315. National Center for Complementary and Alternative Medicine (NCCAM). http://nccam.nih.gov/health/reiki/introduction.htm#hed6 (accessed January 25, 2013).

Lewis, James R. and J. Gordon Melton. *Perspectives on the New Age.* Albany, NY: SUNY Press, 1992.

Leyshon, Dr. Gareth. *Catholic Critique of the Healing Art of Reiki.* Abstract: The Complementary Therapy {A Catholic Critique of the Healing Art of Reiki}. United States Conference of Catholic Bishops, 2009.

McClenton, Rhonda J. *Spirits of the Lesser Gods: A Critical Examination of Reiki and Christ-Centered Healing.* Boca Raton: Dissertation.com, 2005.

Melton, J. Gordon et al. *Chronology of the New Age Movement.* New Age Encyclopedia. 1990. Detroit: Gail Research, 1990. (Taken from a four page section in the New Age Encyclopedia titled (xxxv-xxxviii).

Noebel, David. *Understanding the Times: The Collision of Today's Competing Worldviews* (Rev. 2nd ed). Summit Press, 2006. Compliments of John Stonestreet, David Noebel, and the Christian Worldview Ministry at Summit Ministries. All rights reserved in the original.

O'Mathuna, Donal and Walter L. Lairmore. *Alternative Medicine.* Grand Rapids: Zondervan, 2001, 2007.

Pace, Edward. *Pantheism.* The Catholic Encyclopedia. Vol. 11. New York: Robert Appleton Company, 1911. http://www.newadvent.org/cathen/11447b.html

(accessed January 25, 2013).

Partridge, Christopher. *Introduction to World Religions*. Minneapolis: Fortress Press, 2005.

Pike, Sarah M. *New Age and Neopagan Religions in America*. New York, NY: Columbia University Press, 2004.

R.T. Kendall, *Understanding Theology: The Means of Developing a Healthy Church in the 21st Century.* Scotland: Christian Focus Publishers, 1998. Reprint edition 2000.

Rand, William L. *Reiki: The Healing Touch, First and Second Degree Manual* (Expanded and Revised ed.). Reiki. The International Center for Reiki Training. Vision Publications. 2000.

Reed, David A. "Healing in the Atonement or the Fingers?" paper presented at the Synergy Institute for Leadership, Hong Kong, 2010.

Sire, James. *The Universe Next Door,* 5th ed. Downers Grove, IL: InterVarsity Press, 2009.

Tournier, Paul. *The Healing of Persons*. New York: Harper & Row; Third Edition, 1965.

vanderVaart, S; Gijsen, V; Wildt, S; Koren, G. "A Systematic Review of the Therapeutic Effects of Reiki." *The Journal of Alternative and Complementary Medicine* 15, (2009).

Wakoff, Michael B. "Theosophy." *Routledge Encyclopedia of Philosophy*, 9. New York: Routledge, 1998.

OTHER BOOKS
FROM RANDY CLARK

Changed in a Moment

Deliverance

Essential Guide to Healing

Entertaining Angels

God Can Use Little Ole Me

Healing Unplugged

Lighting Fires

Power, Holiness, and Evangelism

Supernatural Missions

The Healing River and It's Contributing Streams

There is More

MINISTRY MANUALS

Ministry Team Training Manual

Kingdom Foundations:
A School of Healing and Impartation

Empowered: A School of Healing and Impartation

Healing: Medical and Spiritual Perspectives

THE CORE MESSAGE SERIES
FROM RANDY CLARK

Awed By His Grace / Out of the Bunkhouse

Baptism in the Holy Spirit

Biblical Basis for Healing

Christ in You the Hope of Glory / Healing and the Glory

Evangelism Unleashed

Healing is in the Atonement / Power of the Lord's Supper

Learning to Minister Under the Anointing / Healing Ministry in Your Church

Open Heaven / Are You Thirsty

Pressing In / Spend and Be Spent

Thrill of Victory / Agony of Defeat

Words of Knowledge

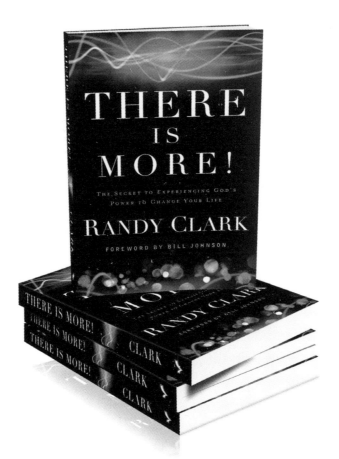

"This is the book that Randy Clark was born to write." - Bill Johnson

In "There Is More", Randy will lay a solid biblical foudation for a theology of impartation as well as take a historical look at the impartation and visitation of the Lord in the Church. This will be combined with many personal testimonies of people who have received an impartation throughout the world and what the lasting fruit has been in their lives. You will be taken on journey throughout the world and see for yourself the lasting fruit that is taking place in the harvest field - particularly in Mozambique. This release of power is not only about phenomena of the Holy Spirit, it is about its ultimate effect on evangelism and missions. Your heart will be stirred for more as you read this book.

For this and other books go to: globalawakeningstore.com

"When I read this, my spirit shouted 'Yes and Amen!' May Randy's personal journey build faith to believe that God heals today."

Dr. Heidi Baker Founder of IRIS Global.

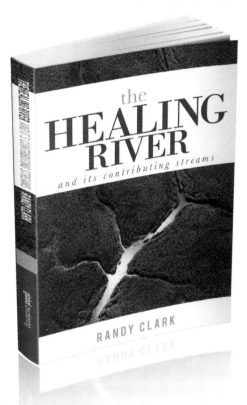

It is no wonder there is so little real expectancy for receiving healing through prayer in many of the churches of America and Western Europe. Pastors have been trained in unbelief regarding healing through prayer by the very seminaries established to train them for ministry. However, Randy would argue that history and current moves of God confirms that He still heals and that the Church is still active in the healing ministry.

In **The Healing River and Its Contributing Streams**, Randy discusses the various Christian healing streams, their impact on the church today, and dispels the myths and attitudes we have towards them bringing unity to the entire Body of Christ. Rediscover the message of the Kingdom and experience the power of God through healing prayer.

LEARN TO MINISTER AS JESUS DID.

Do you feel a stirring in your heart to take the next step in preparation for ministry? Do you want to see healing and deliverance operating in your own life? Join us for one of our online classes in the areas of Physical Healing, Deliverance or Inner Healing. The Christian Healing Certification Program (CHCP) is a great option to expand your ministry training right from the comfort of your home.

No Prior training necessary

Courses are available to fit your schedule

Small and personal classes of 15-17 students per class

It's easy and can be done right from home

Economical and inexpensive

Join a community of online students from all over the world

For more information or to register, visit our website at **www.healingcertification.com** or call 717.796.9866 X124.

BECOME WHO YOU WERE MADE TO BE.
GLOBAL SCHOOL OF SUPERNATURAL MINISTRY

FROM THE FIRST TIME we encounter the King our heart's cry is answered with a resounding "yes!" We are created to take risks and dive deeply into the journey of following Christ. Come to *the Global School of Supernatural Ministry* and you will be empowered to bravely leap into the unknown, as you more intimately know the Creator.

ONSITE • ONLINE • SUMMER INTENSIVE

FOR MORE INFORMATION AND TO APPLY:
GSSM.GLOBALAWAKENING.COM OR 866-AWAKENING EXT:123

Do you hunger for more?

- more power, more glory, more transformation, more of Jesus? Randy Clark has been taking teams to minster to the nations for years. Many lives, both those native to the host country and those on the international team, have been transformed by the power and presence of God. Come with us and experience the fruit for yourselves.

You can learn more and get the latest updates on all of our trips at:

imt.globalawakening.com

If you have additional questions or you would like to register for a trip, you can use the online forms or call us at:

1-866-Awakening

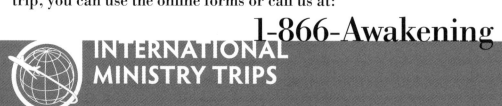

Based in Mechanicsburg, PA, the Apostolic Network of Global Awakening is a teaching, healing and impartation ministry with a heart for the nations. Founded in 1994 by Randy Clark after his involvement with the Toronto Airport Christian Fellowship revival, the ministry exists to fulfill the biblical commissions of Jesus:

As you go preach, saying the Kingdom of heaven is at hand. Heal the sick, cleanse the lepers, raise the dead, cast out demons. Freely you have received, freely give
(Matthew 10:7-8).

For a schedule of upcoming events and conferences, or to purchase other products from Global Awakening, please visit our website at: **globalawakening.com**

PARTNERS

RIGHT NOW, when a kingdom perspective is most needed, Randy's vision is to equip the body by lighting fires, building bridges and casting vision. It is a demanding call on his life and the expansion and explosive growth in the ministries of Global Awakening only continues by the faithful support of those who invest their time and resources to support Randy's vision.

The vision of Global Awakening is dependent on the prayers and financial support of the Global Awakening Partners. You may not be able to go everywhere Randy goes, but you can share in the joy and heavenly reward of changed lives through the Global Awakening ministry. Whether you are on the front lines of battle or connected with the vision through your partnership, together we share the rewards and blessings.

ALL PARTNERS RECEIVE THE FOLLOWING BENEFITS:

- Monthly Partner Newsletter
- Monthly Prayer Theme Support
- Partner Website Access
- Annual Global Awakening Partner Lanyard
- Preferred Conference Registration
- Complimentary Services at Global Events

FIRE STARTER BENEFITS:
At least $25.00 per month or $300 annually

Benefits include:
10% off bookstore at approved Global Awakening Events, and 10% off all Global Awakening events and webcast.

BRIDGE BUILDER BENEFITS:
At least $50.00 per month or $600 annually

Additional Benefits include:
No application fee to GSSM, 25% off all Global Awakening events and webcast, plus benefits from previous tier.

GLOBAL VISION CASTER BENEFITS:
At least $100.00 per month or $1000 annually

Additional Benefits include: Early access to Voice of the Prophets and Voice of the Apostles, 50% off all Global Awakening events and webcast, plus benefits from previous tiers.

MASTER'S COMMISSION BENEFITS:
At least $500.00 per month or $5000 annually

Additional Benefits include: 25% off an international ministry trip, Global Awakening events and webcast are FREE, plus benefits from previous tiers.

PRESIDENT'S COUNCIL BENEFITS:
At least $1000.00 per month or $10,000 annually

Additional Benefits include: 50% off an international ministry trip, President's Council Personal Services, plus benefits from previous tiers.

---

to find out more about our partners program contact us at:

PARTNERS.GLOBALAWAKENING.COM
OR
1-866-AWAKENING.COM EXT: 121

The Apostolic Network of Global Awakening is a missional network of churches and ministries uniting to advance the Kingdom of God. Together we are capable of doing more than we ever could apart. To that end, our Network aims to be a connection point for the senior pastors of churches and the senior leaders of itinerant ministries. Through the Apostolic Network, we are bringing together a company of men and women equipped to do Kingdom work across the globe. In addition to simple community, the Network provides resources and further training opportunities for those who bring their churches and ministries under our covering.
For more information visit http://globalawakening.com/network/about-network

Notes: